God's Grand Story
His Word.
Your Life.

A
Six-Week
Adventure
in the
Old Testament

By Walk Thru the Bible

WALK
THRU ᴛʜᴇ
BIBLE®

TAKE A WALK. CHANGE THE WORLD.

TAKE A WALK. CHANGE THE WORLD.

Walk Thru the Bible
4201 North Peachtree Road
Atlanta, GA 30341-1207
1.800.361.6131

Visit us at **www.walkthru.org**

HOW TO USE THE OLD TESTAMENT GUIDEBOOK

For the next six weeks, you'll be going on an adventure through the Old Testament.

Here's how to get the most out of your experience:

On your own, read the pages titled **Your Quiet Time**. These short daily lessons introduce the week's teaching and help you better understand God's Word. The **Reflection** questions encourage you to internalize God's truth. The **Bottom Line** section provides a concise summary of what you've read. The **Pray** section prompts you to talk to God about how what you've read intersects with your everyday life.

Then, with your small group or Sunday school class, watch the video that accompanies each session of God's Grand Story. As you do you'll see the beauty and wonder of creation as well as the world's brokenness and pain. You'll meet prophets and spies, good kings and bad kings. You'll learn about God's holy character and His compassionate heart.

After each video, you'll spend some time with your group or class discussing what you've watched and read. This is a great opportunity to both share with and learn from others.

Our prayer is that this six-week experience will have a long-term impact in your life. We want you to understand what God's Grand Story means to you personally as you fall deeper in love with God and His Word.

God's Grand Story: His Word. Your Life.

Leader's Notes are located at **www.walkthru.org/ggsot**

Introduction

1. BEGINNINGS
Why do we exist? Where did we come from? What is our purpose? Nearly everyone wrestles with these questions because we long to understand the meaning of life. The Bible gives us many of those answers in its very first book: Genesis.

2. WANDERINGS
Life is a journey, and our story begins in captivity. Like Israel, we need deliverance, a miraculous exodus that sets us free. God provides that to those who cry out to Him and accept His plan, but even then we may spend years navigating the wilderness in front of us. When we trust Him, He gets us to our promised land.

3. PROMISED LAND
Throughout Israel's history, we will see the opportunities promised in the wilderness fulfilled when the nation keeps its end of the covenant. And though God is always faithful even when His people aren't, we will see them miss the promised opportunities when they betray the covenant.

4. UNITED KINGDOM
What is the kingdom of God? This world has not experienced the fullness of His reign since Eden, but we get glimpses of it in Scripture and even in our own lives. One of those glimpses is in the monarchy that developed after the time of the judges. It was never perfect but it would give us that glimpse—hints of what God's greater kingdom will look like one day.

5. DIVIDED KINGDOM
For a brief moment in time, the chosen people had shown signs of their potential glory. But like Adam and Eve in the garden, they fell. And fell again. And again and again. Like the rest of us, they sought sustenance, significance, and meaning in life. But also like many of us, they sought it in the wrong places, wandering from God until He gets our attention.

6. CAPTIVITY AND THE COMING KINGDOM
The consequences of sin are painful, sometimes even devastating. But God never delivers a painful message to His own people without following it with a message of hope. After a long and agonizing exile, the people of God return to Him, and quite a few even return to Jerusalem.

God's **Grand** Story

His Word.
Your Life.

THE GUIDEBOOK
OLD TESTAMENT VERSION

TABLE *of* CONTENTS

DIVIDED KINGDOM

2 Kings 12-25
2 Chronicles 10-36
Isaiah
Jeremiah
Lamentations
Hosea
Joel
Amos
Obadiah
Jonah
Micah
Nahum
Habakkuk
Zephaniah

UNITED KINGDOM

1 & 2 Samuel
1 Kings 1-11
1 Chronicles
2 Chronicles 1-9
Psalms
Proverbs
Ecclesiastes
Song of Songs

CAPTIVITY & THE COMING KINGDOM

Ezra
Nehemiah
Esther
Ezekiel
Daniel
Haggai
Zechariah
Malachi

Creation and Fall

Genesis 1-5

Read Genesis 1:27-31; 3:1-19

So God created mankind in his own image, in the image of God he created them; male and female he created them. (Genesis 1:27 NIV)

Everything God made was good. He said so Himself—repeatedly. The rhythm of light and darkness, the position of the planets and stars, the ecosystem teeming with life, the man made in His image . . . everything. Well, everything except the fact that initially, the man was all alone. He needed a partner. So out of man's own flesh came woman—also made in the image of God. They could relate to God heart to heart, mind to mind, spirit to spirit. They could relate to each other in a way that would reflect greater mysteries to be revealed one day. And together, they could fulfill their God-given mission on earth.

God had not given many specific instructions—apparently this relational God was mainly interested in enjoying the company of His image-bearers in the cool of the evening and letting them enjoy each other's company in His garden— but He did forbid them to eat from one particular tree. As often happens with human beings, the forbidden became the focus. The lying serpent told Eve they "surely" would not die from eating the fruit, as God had said, but would rather become "like God"—as though these image-bearers weren't already like Him. And they would know the difference between good and evil, which apparently hadn't been necessary for them to know if they simply listened to God. So she ate the fruit and gave it to Adam to eat too. And everything changed.

There are consequences for every decision, and we've been experiencing the consequences of this one ever since. Adam and Eve lost paradise. Death entered the world—their oldest son killed his brother—and so did the frustration of hard labor and traumatic labor pains. Envy, strife, hostility, and selfish pride began to flourish outside the garden. But a cryptic prophecy to the serpent would now direct history, though it would take millennia to unfold. The woman's offspring and the serpent's agenda would clash, and the former would crush the latter.

REFLECTION

- When in your life have you seen fleeting, beautiful hints of Eden—of the world as it was meant to be? What evidence do you see of all the evil in the world foretold after the fall? What evidence do you see (maybe even in the news this week) of the animosity between the kingdom of God and the evil agenda of the serpent?
- In what ways do the stories of creation and fall explain the purpose of your life? In what ways do they explain the obstacles you face in fulfilling your purpose?
- When in your life have you been most tempted to question God's goodness? How does the battle to believe that God is good play out in your own relationship with Him? in your current circumstances? in your dreams and goals and prayers? What is at stake in this battle?

NOTES/JOURNAL

_____
_____
_____
_____
_____
_____
_____
_____
_____
_____
_____
_____
_____
_____
_____
_____
_____
_____
_____
_____
_____
_____
_____

BOTTOM LINE

God is good. Creation proves that, the fall distorts our perception of that truth, and all of life is shaped by how willing we are to trust God's goodness and relate to Him on that basis.

PRAY for a greater awareness of God's goodness, the needs of your family, the concerns of your heart.

Judgment and Division

Genesis 6-11

Read Genesis 6:5-8; 11:1-9

The Lord regretted that he had made human beings on the earth, and his heart was deeply troubled. . . . But Noah found favor in the eyes of the Lord.
(Genesis 6:6, 8 NIV)

God experiences grief. We aren't sure what to make of that, especially if we believe what Scripture says about His foresight and unchanging nature. Why would He, knowing how every situation will unfold, proceed with something that would lead to regret? Does God really change His mind? That's how He is portrayed in the story of the flood. He lamented that He ever made human beings, yet He took pleasure in Noah and his family. Through a devastating flood, He delivered Noah's family and preserved each animal species so the world could begin again. This portrait of deliverance points to a greater, more ultimate judgment and salvation later in Scripture, but it tells a lot about God right from the start. He loves His creation; He hates pride, rebellion, and corruption; He judges harshly even when it grieves Him to do so; and even a small remnant is worth preserving. In the end, a promise signified by a rainbow points to His commitment to pursue His good purposes all the way to fulfillment.

Much later, after the population had been replenished, a unified but proud people on the plains of Shinar attempted the ultimate in human achievement. They wanted to ascend to heaven and display their own glory—to "make a name for themselves." God had to "come down" even to notice their greatest accomplishments, but He nevertheless saw the need to thwart them. They weren't obeying His mandate to fill the earth and subdue it. What's more, instead of having humble and dependent hearts, their arrogant sense of self-sufficiency made it impossible for them to have a relationship with God! God mercifully intervened. He diversified their language so they could no longer understand one another. One day that diversity would glorify Him, but for the time it simply kept them from glorifying themselves. They had to scatter. Now His relationship with humanity would shift from the universal to the particular. He divided the world into nations, and He then began to shape one of His own.

REFLECTION

- In Genesis 6 and 11, we see God described in human-like terms. The flood story shows God full of grief and regret. The Tower of Babel incident depicts Him almost as surprised and needing to react hastily. How do you reconcile these portraits with other statements in the Bible that show God to be all-knowing and in control of all things? How do these pictures help you relate to God?
- What is it about pride that elicits such a strong response from God? How would you explain pride to a third-grader? In what areas of your life are you tempted to be independent, to take charge (and push God aside)?

NOTES/JOURNAL

_____

_____

_____

_____

_____

_____

_____

_____

_____

_____

_____

_____

_____

_____

_____

_____

_____

_____

_____

_____

BOTTOM LINE

Every human attempt to live independently from God fails. But He gives grace to those who humbly look to Him for help, direction, strength, and life.

PRAY for greater humility, a deeper desire to seek God's truth, more love for Him, and that your family members might come to know God in a deeply personal way.

Abraham and Isaac

Genesis 12:1–25:18

Read Genesis 12:1-3; 15:1-6; 22:1-18

Abram believed the LORD, and the LORD counted him as righteous because of his faith. (Genesis 15:6 NLT)

Terah intended to move his family—including son Abram, Abram's wife Sarai, and grandson Lot—from Ur (near the mouth of the Tigris and Euphrates) to Canaan (present-day Israel), but they settled down about halfway there in Haran. But when Abram was 75, God told him to move. Where? That information would come later. So Abram (later Abraham), Sarai (later Sarah), and their nephew Lot left Haran and eventually ended up in Canaan.

God had given Abraham and Sarah a staggering promise: they would have countless descendants who would bless all the peoples of the earth. But Abraham and Sarah had a big problem: they were childless and well past the childbearing years. After more than a decade of waiting, Abraham and Sarah tried themselves to make God's promise come true. Abraham fathered a child through his wife's maid, Hagar. Though God promised to bless this child—Ishmael—He made it clear that the child of the promise was yet to be born. He reassured Abraham that his descendants would come through his and Sarah's biological son. Twenty-five years after the promise was first given by God, Isaac was born. Abraham was 100! Sarah was 90! Imagine their joy! And imagine their pain some years later when Abraham was asked to sacrifice Isaac on a mountain. Abraham obeyed, and God intervened to prevent the sacrifice at the last moment, providing a nearby ram as an offering.

Though Abraham certainly had missteps, moments of questioning, and mistaken attempts to help God's promises along, the testimony of Scripture is that he beautifully models the kind of faith on which God builds His kingdom. That means that when God's calling leads us to unknown places, when His promises take painfully long years to come to pass, and when He asks us to make excruciating sacrifices, nothing unusual is going on. This is normal in His kingdom. This is how He grows our trust, develops our perseverance, and equips us for significant kingdom purposes. And, as He did with Abraham, He counts us righteous because of our faith.

REFLECTION

- What do you admire most about Abraham and Sarah? Where are you being stretched in your faith? Are there any areas of your life where you sense God nudging you to move out into the unknown?
- How would your relationship with God be tested if you had to wait 25 years for a promise to be fulfilled? How would your relationship with Him be tested if He asked you to sacrifice that promise after it had been fulfilled?
- Hebrews 11:6 says it is impossible to please God without faith. Why do you think God places such a high priority on faith?

NOTES/JOURNAL

_____

_____

_____

_____

_____

_____

_____

_____

_____

_____

_____

_____

_____

_____

_____

_____

_____

_____

_____

_____

_____

_____

BOTTOM LINE

God's plan to rescue and restore His beloved creatures begins with a promise and requires His followers to live lifestyles of deep, persistent faith.

PRAY as Jesus' disciples prayed, "Increase our faith" (Luke 17:5). Ask God to show you things in your life that stand in the way of you following Him more fully.

Jacob

Genesis 25:19–36:43

Read Genesis 28:10-22; 32:22-29

"Your name will no longer be Jacob," He said. "It will be Israel because you have struggled with God and with men and have prevailed." (Genesis 32:28 HCSB)

Isaac and his wife, Rebekah, had twin sons: Esau and Jacob. Esau was born first, but with his brother Jacob hanging on to his heel—a picture of the life they would lead. Esau was a man's man, but he was also undisciplined and rash, trading all his advantages as the firstborn son of Isaac for one bowl of stew. Jacob was his mother's favorite, and she helped him carry out a plan to deceive Isaac into giving him the special blessing reserved for the oldest son. Old and blind, Isaac fell for it. Meaning to bless Esau, he blessed Jacob instead. The deception enraged Esau, and Jacob had to flee for his life. He went to his family's home country, fell in love with Rachel, one of his uncle's daughters, and worked for seven years to marry her. But the deceiver was deceived into marrying Leah, the other daughter, first. The end result was two wives for 14 years of labor.

That's how Jacob ended up with 12 sons and at least one daughter. The sisters' jealousy incited a childbearing competition: they even offered their maids to Jacob to increase their offspring. Eventually, Jacob left with his wives and children to return to Canaan but was terrified by Esau's possible reaction. Did Esau still want to kill Jacob? Jacob sent extravagant gifts ahead to smooth the way. The gifts, however, were not needed. Esau welcomed him with open arms. Jacob and his family—Abraham's early descendants—settled in the land where the children of Israel would one day be a nation.

Jacob encountered God several times in his life, but perhaps the two most significant occasions were when he was fleeing Canaan and when he was returning years later. In the first, he had a dream in which he saw the angels of God descending and ascending on a ladder or stairway. He woke up marveling that God had been there without him knowing it, and he renamed the place Bethel— house of God. Years later, having prospered and proliferated in a distant land, he returned home. The night before he would meet his brother Esau again, he wrestled with God, refusing to let go unless God blessed him. Many might fear God's wrath in this situation, but God blessed Jacob, renamed him Israel, and honored his striving with both God and man as the kind of attitude on which godly nations are built.

REFLECTION

- Why do you think God established Israel through a family situation filled with deception, envy, competition, and friction? Should such flaws and weaknesses disqualify us from fulfilling His purposes? Why or why not?
- What do you make of this strange scene in which Jacob "wrestled with God"? In what ways have you wrestled with God? Have you felt guilty or reluctant to engage with Him this way? Why does God welcome the opportunity to interact with us like this?

NOTES/JOURNAL

_____

_____

_____

_____

_____

_____

_____

_____

_____

_____

_____

_____

_____

_____

_____

_____

_____

_____

_____

_____

_____

_____

BOTTOM LINE

God is not limited by our imperfections or weaknesses. In fact, He works them into His plan, overcomes them, and blesses us for responding to Him with faith and persistence.

PRAY for some of your family's dysfunctions; confess any envy, sibling rivalry, or tension; ask for the courage to engage in healing conversations with family members.

Joseph

Genesis 37-50

Read Genesis 37:2-11; 41:37-41; 50:14-21

"You planned evil against me; God planned it for good to bring about the present result—the survival of many people." (Genesis 50:20 HCSB)

Perhaps Joseph was naive, or maybe even a little cocky. Whatever the reason, he told his brothers that, according to his God-given dreams, they would bow down to him one day. That only increased the intensity of their jealousy and anger toward him, and they couldn't keep it in. They conspired to kill their father Jacob's favored son, then reconsidered and sold him to some traders who were on their way to Egypt. Joseph would spend the rest of his life in Egypt.

But Joseph's dreams weren't dead. God favored Joseph as a slave in Potiphar's house, though his master's wife's attempt to seduce him resulted in Joseph being falsely accused and imprisoned. Then God favored Joseph as a prisoner, though a palace cupbearer forgot to put in a good word for him. Eventually, his ability to hear from God and interpret dreams were needed in Pharaoh's court. His divinely inspired insight would spare a nation from the devastation of a famine, and he was elevated in the short span of one day from prison to second in power in the land. When famine finally struck, Joseph's brothers came to Egypt for assistance. He put them through an elaborate test to see if they had changed over the years, and they passed. He revealed his identity, his brothers rejoiced and hoped for his forgiveness, and Jacob moved from Canaan to Egypt to live with the son he thought had died. After years of patience, faithfulness, and integrity, Joseph's dreams came to pass.

Through Joseph, God demonstrated His commitment to provide for His people and His desire to bless a pagan nation through one of Abraham's descendants, as promised. He also proved that He can not only work around and through the kind of dysfunction rampant in Jacob's family, He can also work around and through the worst sort of treachery inflicted on one of His children. Upon revealing his dreams, Joseph was carried in exactly the opposite direction from their fulfillment. Or so it seemed. Yet in the evil intended by Joseph's brothers, God worked His plan out to perfection.

REFLECTION

- Do you ever worry that you might have missed God's plans for your life? In what ways might Joseph's story reassure you?
- Why do you think God favored Joseph and kept elevating him to second position in every situation? What fears and doubts would you have wrestled with if you had been in his situation for years of waiting?
- How was Joseph able to forgive his brothers? What attitudes and perspectives helped him get over their offense? Is there a situation or relationship in your life where forgiveness is needed and where you're finding it hard to let go of your bitterness?

NOTES/JOURNAL

_____

_____

_____

_____

_____

_____

_____

_____

_____

_____

_____

_____

_____

_____

_____

_____

_____

_____

_____

_____

BOTTOM LINE

God's purposes are not thwarted by the evil actions of people. He is always will-ing and able to put His people in position to apply His solutions to society's needs.

PRAY for the grace to forgive those who have wronged you, and for the wis-dom to see how God can use past hurts to bless others through you.

Jesus in Genesis

Though Jesus doesn't appear overtly in Scripture until the New Testament, the Old Testament contains all kinds of hints and pointers and previews of the coming Savior. He is behind the scenes in . . .

1. Genesis 1. According to John 1:1-5 and Colossians 1:15-17, all things were created through Him.
2. Genesis 3:15. The prophecy of the offspring of the woman crushing the serpent's head and the serpent striking His heel refers to the cross and resurrection of Christ.
3. Melchizedek. In Genesis 14, a mysterious priest of the Most High God, called the "king of Salem" (king of shalom, or prince of peace), appears with bread and wine to bless Abraham and receive an offering from him. Melchizedek is at least a picture of Jesus, if not Jesus Himself.
4. Isaac. In Genesis 22, Isaac carrying the wood for the sacrifice up Mount Moriah is a beautiful portrayal of the cross of Christ. The father's beloved son is offered up as a sacrifice, yet received back as if raised from certain death.
5. Jacob's ladder. In Genesis 28, Jacob saw angels ascending and descending on a stairway. Jesus compared Himself to this doorway to heaven in John 1:51.
6. Joseph. The story of Jacob's (Israel's) favored son can be seen as a remarkable picture of Jesus—the father's beloved son making offensive claims, being stripped of his clothes (which are dipped in blood), cast into a pit, raised out of the pit, sold for pieces of silver, rejected by his brothers while ministering among Gentiles, until one day in the end his own people finally recognize him and bow before him, and Israel is saved.

Throughout His story, God is laying a foundation for Jesus and foreshadowing His incarnation—even from the very beginning.

NOTES/JOURNAL

_____

_____

_____

_____

_____

_____

_____

_____

_____

_____

_____

_____

_____

_____

_____

_____

_____

_____

_____

_____

_____

_____

_____

LOOK AHEAD

The journey to Egypt began as Israel's salvation from famine. It morphs into Israel's captivity for four centuries. Joseph delivered them into Egypt. Who will deliver them out? The story continues with a dramatic rescue and, as is often the case with God, long years of waiting and longing for a promise.

OVERVIEW

"In the beginning, God . . ." We don't know much about reality before this universe was created, but we do know that God always has been and always will be. He is timeless. According to Genesis, God merely spoke and everything came into being. Light, substance, life in all its forms . . . He is the author, and everything He created was good—especially human beings, who were crafted in His own image. He gave us a special role to play in this world and blessed us to fill the earth and govern it with Him. But the first humans turned away from God. They chose to go their own independent way, and as a result, sin and its terrible consequences entered the world. The rest of the Bible is the story of how God made restoration possible—how He instituted a plan to forgive sin, reconcile His rebellious creatures to Himself, and begin a new creation within the old one. Even from the beginning, God had a plan. And this plan is still being fulfilled in our lives today.

THE STORY: 4 EVENTS, 4 PEOPLE

Genesis is actually filled with many events and people, but the story hinges on four of each.

EVENTS

1. Creation—God reveals His original design and purposes.
2. Fall—We live in a fallen world because the first humans question God's goodness and rebel against His instructions.
3. Flood—Humanity strays so far from God's purposes that He starts over with one faithful family.
4. Division of nations—Stubbornly banding together against God's revealed will, the inhabitants of earth proudly seek to find glory and significance apart from God. For their own good, He thwarts their plan, separates them by languages, and scatters them throughout the earth.

PEOPLE

1. Abraham—God begins His plan to rescue a sinful world by graciously choosing a man who will simply believe in Him.
2. Isaac—God promises, Abraham and Sarah believe, and Isaac is born—eventually—becoming a picture of Abraham's faith and God's faithfulness.
3. Jacob—He not only encounters God several times, he wrestles with Him. Jacob becomes the father of 12 sons who would form a nation.
4. Joseph—The favored son of Jacob endures a long, excruciating ordeal to become the leader, provider, and protector of his family and to save a region from famine.

WATCH

As you watch the video, focus on the big picture. Ask yourself these questions: What was God's purpose in creation? Why would God's plan for the world allow for the possibility of sin and evil? What does Genesis reveal about God's character and how He wants us to relate to Him?

VIDEO NOTES

_____

_____

_____

_____

_____

_____

VIDEO REFLECTION/GROUP DISCUSSION

Think back about a specific time you doubted the goodness of God. Describe your circumstances.

_____

_____

_____

_____

_____

_____

DIG DEEPER

Genesis offers a different perspective from what we often hear from scientists and philosophers about the big questions of life. It introduces us to the reason we exist (we aren't random, meaningless creatures); the reality of sin (we have hearts that are inclined to rebel against God); both the mercy and holiness of God (He loves us but cannot overlook sin—in fact, He _must_ judge it); God's relentless pursuit of His plan (the centerpiece of which is a relationship with those made in His image); the necessity of faith (we cannot relate to God without it); and the foreshadows of a Savior (in prophecies and pictures throughout the book). These major themes will come up again and again in Scripture and in our lives, and will shape our understanding of God and His story.

CREATION AND FALL

Read Genesis 1:27-28. Nature includes some pretty amazing creatures, but only human beings are said to be made in the very image of God. What does that mean? What are the implications of the fact that humans bear this designation, but other creatures don't?

After the temptation and Adam and Eve's disobedience, God spoke to the serpent, the man, and the woman about the consequences of their decisions. God declared that there would be hostility between the woman and the serpent, promising that the woman's offspring would crush the serpent's head (see Genesis 3:15). What does this pronouncement say about God's heart? Do you think this prophecy was a predesigned purpose or back-up plan? Why?

JUDGMENT AND DIVISION

Read Genesis 6:5-8. What does this passage tell us about the heart of man? What does it reveal about God's righteousness? What's your response to the fact that this passage says God was grieved/sorry/sad that He had made man?

The people of Babel wanted to build a city and a tower reaching into the heavens in order to make a name for themselves and avoid being scattered throughout the earth (Genesis 11:4). What attitudes and insecurities does this reflect? Why would God oppose this plan? In what ways did this plan conflict with His character? How did it conflict with His purposes?

ABRAHAM AND ISAAC

God called Abraham to leave his home and go to a land that he would be shown later. Why do you think God chose Abraham out of all the other people in the world? Why do you think God didn't tell him up front where he would go? What would have been your response if God had told you to pack your stuff, leave everything familiar, and launch out on a journey without giving you an itinerary or detailed plan?

Abraham and Sarah were already old and childless, yet God promised they would have many descendants. How would you feel if you had been given this promise in their situation? What if God made you wait 25 years before making good on His promise?

Genesis 22 is one of those chapters we have a hard time reading. There, God tells Abraham to sacrifice Isaac, his long-awaited beloved son. Why would God ask such a thing? What does Abraham's response reveal about his faith and priorities?

JACOB

Jacob's family would make a great case study in dysfunction: deceptive family members (and also deceptive himself); a brother who wanted to kill him; a marriage under false pretenses; 12 sons born from two wives and two servants engaged in competitive childbearing; and a long night (or decades) of wrestling with God Himself. Yet God gave him a new name and established him as the father of a nation. What does this show us about the kind of people God chooses? How does it encourage you about any obstacles in your life?

JOSEPH

God gave Joseph dreams about his glorious future, and Joseph, perhaps in youthful immaturity, told his brothers, who already hated him for being his father's favorite son. When the brothers betrayed him and sent him in the opposite direction of his dreams, what questions might Joseph have had about his actions? about God's faithfulness? about his future?

Years later, when Joseph was second in command in Egypt, he told his long-lost brothers that what they intended for evil, God had meant for good (Genesis 50:20). What does this tell us about the relationship between adversity and God's purpose for our lives? How does the truth that God is in control of all things, that He is able to orchestrate even bad things for greater good, help us in dealing with hard things or hurtful people?

Wanderings

BEGINNINGS
Genesis

PROMISED LAND
Joshua
Judges
Ruth

WANDERINGS

Exodus
Leviticus
Numbers
Deuteronomy

DIVIDED KINGDOM

2 Kings 12-25
2 Chronicles 10-36
Isaiah
Jeremiah
Lamentations
Hosea
Joel
Amos
Obadiah
Jonah
Micah
Nahum
Habakkuk
Zephaniah

UNITED KINGDOM

1 & 2 Samuel
1 Kings 1-11
1 Chronicles
2 Chronicles 1-9
Psalms
Proverbs
Ecclesiastes
Song of Songs

CAPTIVITY & THE COMING KINGDOM

Ezra
Nehemiah
Esther
Ezekiel
Daniel
Haggai
Zechariah
Malachi

Moses and Pharaoh

Exodus 1-11

Read Exodus 3:1–4:17; 7:1-7

"I have certainly seen the oppression of my people in Egypt. I have heard their cries of distress because of their harsh slave drivers. Yes, I am aware of their suffering. So I have come down to rescue them." (Exodus 3:7-8 NLT)

Moses' mother sent him floating down the Nile in a basket to save his life, and Pharaoh's daughter found him. So the Israelite infant grew up in the royal household as an Egyptian. But he never stopped identifying with his own people. When he defended one Hebrew slave by killing an oppressive Egyptian taskmaster, he ended up having to flee into the desert wilderness. The would-be deliverer seemed to have missed his calling by attempting to do the right thing in the wrong way and at the wrong time. But God wasn't through with Moses. Four decades later, God appeared to him from within a burning bush. He called a very reluctant Moses to return to Egypt and lead his countrymen to freedom. What an assignment—getting the most powerful man in the world to allow his free labor force to simply leave the country!

God's message for Pharaoh through Moses was simple: "Let My people go." Yet there was a greater purpose than mere freedom: "so they can worship Me" (Exodus 7:16, 8:1, 9:1; 9:13). He wanted to relieve their suffering, of course, but more than that, He wanted to draw them into a free and meaningful relationship with Him. This mission wasn't simply about human rights. It served to illustrate God's goal for His fallen world: setting people free from slavery to sin so that they might again know and love and worship Him.

It took 10 divinely sent plagues to convince Pharaoh to let Israel go, and even then he would later have second thoughts. Time and again, God inflicted "natural" disasters on Egypt's population, not because He delights in suffering but in order to prompt repentance. Yet no matter how much Pharaoh was pained and humiliated by each plague, he continued to harden his heart against God, even as God sovereignly ordained his stubbornness. Only when he lost his firstborn son did he relent.

Not only did this series of events birth a nation, it also painted a picture of God's deliverance and the enemy who opposes it. Captives to the fallen human condition, we are the recipients of a great deliverance many centuries after these events. Mankind's stubborn enemy remains; he does not easily let go of his captives. Yet he is no match for the great Deliverer. Those who put their trust in Him cannot be kept in chains.

REFLECTION

- Moses was reluctant to accept God's call, offering excuse after excuse. How would you have felt if God called you into a situation that would probably result in your death if God didn't show up and defend you? What would it take to convince you of God's power?

- The people didn't believe in Moses' mission at first because they were too discouraged from their slavery (Exodus 6:9). Are there any areas of your life in which you're afraid to hope? If so, what? Why is God's good news sometimes hard to believe?
- In what areas do you need to experience freedom?

NOTES/JOURNAL

_____

_____

_____

_____

_____

_____

_____

_____

_____

_____

_____

_____

_____

_____

_____

_____

_____

_____

BOTTOM LINE

God is determined to free His people—even when they don't at first believe His promises or understand His processes.

PRAY for the ability to notice "burning bushes" in your life, and for the courage to obey God's call. Ask God to comfort family members who are struggling to trust His promises.

Passover and the Red Sea

Exodus 12-15

Read Exodus 12:24-36; 13:17-22; 14:10-14, 21-31

*"Do not be afraid. Stand firm and you will see the deliverance the L*ORD *will bring you today. . . . The L*ORD *will fight for you; you need only to be still."*
(Exodus 14:13-14 NIV)

Before the last, decisive plague, God told the Israelites to slaughter one lamb per household and paint its blood on their doorposts. This would be a sign for the angel of death to pass over Jewish homes during the night of the plague. On that night, all the firstborns—of humans and animals alike—would die unless blood was on the home's doorposts. Before the event, God gave very specific instructions, told the people to gather up their possessions and livestock and families, had them prepare food quickly (bread without leaven, for example), and let them know the commemoration of this event would become an annual celebration. And that night, God did just as He had said. Every Egyptian household was filled with wailing.

By this time, Pharaoh was ready for Moses and his people to leave. He'd had enough. He commanded them to leave, and Israel's people left not only with their families and possessions, but also with many of the possessions given to them by the Egyptians. God did not lead them on a direct route to the Promised Land—His people would have encountered enemies and turned back. Instead, He led them on a curious route that would put them at the edge of an impassable sea. And when Pharaoh had a change of heart and sent his army out to pursue the escaping slaves, the people were pinned between two impossible situations. Death looked certain.

But God would not deliver His people into an impossible, deadly situation, in spite of the lament of many of them that He had done exactly that. The presence of God stood between Israel's camp and the advancing army, a powerful wind blew all night on the waters of the sea, Moses lifted his staff, the people crossed the next morning, and then the waters closed over the Egyptian army and destroyed it. Safe on the other side, God's people sang a song of celebration. They were finally free!

REFLECTION

- In the New Testament, Jesus is called our Passover Lamb (see 1 Corinthians 5:7). In what ways do the events described in Exodus 12 foreshadow the coming of Christ?
- Based on the example of the Israelites, what would you say is God's purpose in setting us free from sin and death?
- What seemingly impossible situations are you currently facing? How are you encouraged by the story of Israel's deliverance? What would you say is God's part in your dilemma? What is your part?

NOTES/JOURNAL

_____

_____

_____

_____

_____

_____

_____

_____

_____

_____

_____

_____

_____

_____

_____

_____

_____

_____

_____

_____

_____

BOTTOM LINE

God goes to great lengths to secure our freedom and protect us from our enemies, delivering us through "impossible" situations.

PRAY for a deeper appreciation of what God has done in sending Jesus to rescue you and for God's power to be on display in a seemingly "impossible" situation in your life.

Glory, Covenant, and Presence

Exodus 16–Leviticus 27

Read Exodus 19:16–20:21; 33:12–34:9

"You must be holy because I, the LORD, am holy. I have set you apart from all other people to be my very own." (Leviticus 20:26 NLT)

On the safe side of the Red Sea, the people were led into the wilderness and found themselves in immediate need of provision and protection. God gave them manna from heaven, water from a rock, and a victory over hostile Amalekites—a preview of the kind of protection and provision the Israelites would need and that God would provide during their wilderness years. But soon God turned from their most urgent needs to their more lasting ones: their relationship with Him and each other, their identity as a nation, and their necessary patterns of worship. They were to be a distinct people, holy like their God, a living "show and tell" to the nations around them of God's goodness and grace. For this to happen, they needed to understand how their sin separated them from God's presence, and how the blood of a sacrifice, humbly offered, would make that presence available. God established a sacrificial system, overseen by a priesthood. He prescribed seven symbolic, annual feasts. He gave them precise plans for a tabernacle rich with meaning, at the center of which was an unfathomably holy space. He supplied them with explicit instructions regarding the right (and wrong) ways to approach Him in worship. In all of these He revealed His holy character, His gracious heart, and His good purposes.

Moses found himself functioning as a mediator between God and His people, receiving God's words to give to them and presenting their needs to God. At times, he would have to intercede because of their rebellious and idolatrous ways, which had already begun to manifest. But God showed Moses His glory and committed to see His people all the way into their destiny.

When we think of God's "law," we think of an impossible standard, a code of conduct, and an incredibly complicated system of rituals and sacrifices. From the beginning, the Jewish mind has seen God's law as "instructions" or "sayings," or even the terms of a marriage contract between God and His people. Indeed, His purpose was never to hold us to an impossible standard, but to reveal His character, show us the way to live for our own good, and invite us into a deep relationship with Him. This is why the first four of the Ten Commandments emphasize His love for us and our undivided loyalty to Him. When God is uppermost in our hearts and minds, the stage is set for us to live lives marked by adoration and obedience.

REFLECTION

- What comes to mind when you think of God's law? In what ways does God show that He will have mercy for those who fail to keep it?
- Why do you think it was important to God to establish His presence in the tabernacle in the midst of His people? What does that say about His desire to be with us today?

• How would you describe the glory of God to a friend or coworker? How does this compare to the way God described His own glory in Exodus 34:6-7?

NOTES/JOURNAL

_____

_____

_____

_____

_____

_____

_____

_____

_____

_____

_____

_____

_____

_____

_____

_____

_____

_____

_____

BOTTOM LINE

God has to make extraordinary provisions in order to be able to fellowship with fallen humanity, and He does everything necessary to make it possible.

PRAY for reverence for God. Ask Him to show you areas in your life that are dishonoring to Him. When He does, confess these things and receive the forgiveness that is available to every child of God through the work of Jesus Christ.

12 Spies
Numbers 1-14

Read Numbers 13:17–14:25

"Tell Aaron and his sons how you are to bless the Israelites. Say to them: May Yahweh bless you and protect you; may Yahweh make His face shine on you, and be gracious to you; may Yahweh look with favor on you and give you peace. In this way they will pronounce My name over the Israelites, and I will bless them." (Numbers 6:23-27 HCSB)

After a national census and some further legal instructions, human nature—something all the rules in the world can't fix—began to display its ugly side. The people of God complained about food and hardship, and just about everything else. This prompted Moses to ask God for relief. The Lord gave him a plan for establishing a group of 70 assistants (called "elders"). God provided quail to satisfy the people's desire for meat; then He sent a plague to express His displeasure with their faithless grumbling. Things only got worse. Moses' own siblings, Aaron and Miriam, rebelled against his leadership, and were judged severely for being critical of God's servant.

But the key turning point in this period was the scouting of the Promised Land. Moses sent 12 spies into Canaan, not to determine whether it was vulnerable to attack, but to learn about the cities and the agricultural conditions. Ten of the spies, however, came back with a very pessimistic assessment of the people of the land. They were too big and too strong. Clearly God had led them toward certain disaster! And the spies were so convincing in their reports of the giant Canaanites, and their predictions of doom, that they convinced the people to abandon any thought of moving forward. The faith-filled exhortations of the other two spies, Joshua and Caleb, fell on deaf ears.

God was so displeased with their display of unbelief that He offered to wipe out the entire nation and start over with Moses. Moses passed this "divine test" by pleading on behalf of God's people and expressing concern for God's reputation. In the end, God sentenced the entire nation to wander the wilderness south of Canaan for the next 40 years (one year for every day the spies had been in the land). Only after all the doubters died off (that is, everyone 20 years and older with the exception of Joshua and Caleb) would the next generation of Israelites be able to enter the Promised Land. What a sobering picture of the high price of unbelief and disobedience!

REFLECTION
- Why do you think complaining is so offensive to God? On a scale of 1-10 (with 1 being "never" and 10 being "all the time"), how would you rate yourself as a complainer?
- What did the desire of some Israelites to return to Egypt say about their trust in God's nature? What did they expect the journey to be like?
- In what areas are you tempted to fear the "giants in the land"? What attitude does God want you to have toward the apparent obstacles in your life?

• Read Hebrews 6:10-11. What are the attitudes we must possess if we are to inherit God's promises?

NOTES/JOURNAL

_____

_____

_____

_____

_____

_____

_____

_____

_____

_____

_____

_____

_____

_____

_____

_____

_____

_____

_____

_____

BOTTOM LINE
God never honors unbelief or complaints about circumstances. Instead He expects us to focus on His promises and trust His character no matter what our situation.

PRAY that God would help you cultivate a spirit of contentment. Ask Him to grow your faith and for the courage to take risky steps of obedience today.

The Wilderness Experience

Numbers 15–Deuteronomy 34

Read Numbers 21:4-9; Deuteronomy 6:1-19

"Hear, O Israel: The LORD our God, the LORD is one. Love the LORD your God with all your heart and with all your soul and with all your strength." (Deuteronomy 6:4-5 NIV)

The pattern of discontentment, complaining, rebellion, and God's judgment continued. God dealt with rebels harshly and repeatedly proved His support for Moses and the leaders He had established. He caused Aaron's staff to blossom. He opened up the ground to swallow a faction of antagonists. He protected the wandering nation from the curses of Balaam, a prophet-for-hire who, despite his desire to curse Israel, could only bless them when he opened his mouth. But soon after, many of the men were seduced by Moabite women and joined in their pagan sacrifices. They too experienced God's wrath. The nation called to be different from all others was repeatedly purged of spiritual rebels. After one outburst of impatience, God sent snakes to bite the offenders, and only by looking at a bronze serpent Moses made and lifted high into the air could someone who was bitten survive. Even Moses became impatient once, striking a rock in anger in order to get water to come from it as before. Water did flow, but Moses' failure to treat God as holy in the presence of the people resulted in him being forbidden to enter the Promised Land. Like others of his generation, Moses would die before the journey ended.

But Moses would live long enough to prepare his successor—Joshua, chosen by God to be the next leader—and to reiterate all the essentials of God's instructions to the next generation. In fact, that's what Deuteronomy is—the "second law." Moses recounted much of Israel's history and reminded the people of their unique calling and relationship with God. At its core, the relationship is a matter of loving Him with all of one's being and expressing that love in every area of life. If they cared about His instructions and lived by them, they would be blessed in every way. If not, they would experience the consequences of disobedience, including famine, ill health, and defeat at the hands of enemies. This covenant of blessing and curse forms a grid for understanding much of the rest of the Old Testament—Israel experiences both the blessings of obedience and the consequences of disobedience in the following centuries. And the chief offense coming up repeatedly would be idolatry. False worship would be their downfall again and again because above all, a relationship with God is a matter of loving Him above all else.

REFLECTION

- What does it look like to love God with all your heart, soul, and strength? In what ways does this kind of all-encompassing love shape our attitudes, words, and actions?
- Where do you see yourself in the attitudes, choices, and actions of the Israelites as they wandered about the wilderness?

NOTES/JOURNAL

BOTTOM LINE

In God's plans, the journey is as significant as the destination. More important than when we get there is who we are when we arrive.

PRAY for the grace to love God with all you are and have. Ask God to help you cultivate an attitude of gratitude (instead of a spirit of grumbling).

Jesus in the Wanderings

Just as Genesis presented several pictures of Jesus, so do the next four books of the Bible. He is behind the scenes in . . .

1. The Passover. Just as God spared every household with lamb's blood on its doorposts, so He passes over (that is, forgives) every person who trusts in the blood of Jesus (the "Lamb of God," John 1:29, 36) for the forgiveness of sin.
2. The tabernacle and the ark of the covenant. John 1:14 says that Jesus dwelled among us—literally "tabernacled" with us—and a study of the materials and layout of the tabernacle and the ark points to many parallels between God's presence in the tabernacle and His presence in Jesus.
3. The red heifer and the scapegoat. Numbers 19 speaks of a red cow to be sacrificed outside the camp for purification from death, which some early Christians saw as a symbol of Jesus, who was sacrificed outside the city to deliver us from death; and Leviticus 16 speaks of a scapegoat that is driven out into the wilderness bearing the sins of the people.
4. Manna from heaven and water from a rock. In John 6:35-58, Jesus referred to Himself as the true manna from heaven; and in John 7:37-39, He portrays Himself as the rock from which living water flows. (See also 1 Corinthians 10:4.)
5. The prophet like Moses. In Deuteronomy 18:15 and 18, Moses prophesies a future prophet like him that all must listen to.
6. The bronze serpent. In Numbers 21, Moses lifted up a bronze serpent—a picture of the curse—to which all could look and be saved. Jesus applied this image to Himself in John 3:14-15.

NOTES/JOURNAL

_____

_____

_____

_____

_____

_____

_____

_____

_____

_____

_____

_____

_____

_____

_____

_____

_____

_____

_____

_____

LOOK AHEAD

The journey out of Egypt was costly and dramatic, and the years between deliverance and the Promised Land were full of obstacles and missed opportunities. But the education God's people received in the wilderness has trained them for the challenges they will face in the Promised Land. As the next generation prepares to enter, they are reminded of what's most important—a lesson they will forget and remember many times in the following centuries.

OVERVIEW

Grace and discipline. Some might argue that one shows God's love and the other His anger. But a closer look reveals that they are both expressions of His love. Just as good parents provide for needs (and many wants), protect and/or rescue from harm, teach and guide in the right way to live, and address wrong behavior, so God deals with His children. In Exodus we see Him delivering His people from slavery and rescuing them from their enemies. In Leviticus we see God giving explicit instructions on the right way to live and worship. In Numbers we witness God guiding, providing for, and disciplining His wayward people. In Deuteronomy we hear Him patiently reminding the next generation of Israelites of how to live lives that honor God, bless the world, and bring personal fulfillment. God's goal in all of this? To bring them (and us) into a right and intimate relationship with Himself.

THE STORY: LIFE IN THE WILDERNESS

When **Exodus** opens, Jacob's family has grown over 400 years into a small nation, a nation of slaves. God prepares their deliverance from Egypt through the birth of a child named Moses. Spared from mass infanticide, Moses grows up in Egypt's royal household. Many years later, while in exile, Moses encounters God in a burning bush and is called to deliver His people. Through a series of 10 devastating plagues, God convinces the stubborn Pharaoh to let the Israelites go. In a dramatic picture of salvation—the Passover coupled with the miraculous crossing of the Red Sea—God liberates the nation of Israel! Moses then leads them to Mount Sinai where they will officially become God's covenant people.

At its core, the covenant God makes with the Israelites (**Exodus** and **Leviticus**) is a commitment that He will be their God and they will be His special possession. They are to love Him above all and worship Him alone. This agreement is meant to function more like marriage vows, and less like a system of do's and don'ts. The so-called "Law of Moses" is comprehensive in that it covers all of life. It not only features a moral code but also dietary and health guidelines. It gives instructions for Israel's religious leaders in how to carry out various sacrifices. It stipulates special days of worship and annual festivals for celebrating God's goodness. It also contains detailed plans for Israel's central worship facility (called the tabernacle). In that place God promises to dwell, His presence is signified by a cloud during the day and a column of fire at night.

The book of **Numbers** begins with the people taking a census and then setting out for Canaan. This was a journey that should have taken, at most, a few weeks. It ends up taking 40 years! The journey would have been shorter, but when Moses sends 12 spies from their camp in Kadesh into Canaan, only two, Joshua and Caleb, come back with any faith intact. The other 10 question God's ability to bring His people into the Promised Land. So this faithless generation will wander and complain, though they are fed by miraculous manna from heaven and given water from a rock in the desert. They will fight battles, face temptations, and deal with internal strife and rebellions. But God will prepare their children to inherit the promise. When the time comes to enter, Moses reiterates the people's history and law to the next generation in **Deuteronomy**. Moses himself will not be allowed to enter because of a moment of rash disobedience. He dies. But God will take His people into the land as He has promised.

WATCH

As you watch the video, think about how Israel's story overlaps with yours. Has God set you free to worship Him? How has He provided for you in your "wilderness"? Do you waver between faith and unbelief as you consider the promises He has given you? How are you learning to follow God's leading?

VIDEO NOTES

_____

_____

_____

_____

_____

_____

VIDEO REFLECTION/GROUP DISCUSSION

Have you gone through any wilderness experiences yourself, and how did you do so? Or do you know someone who went through a wilderness experience and came out stronger by faith?

_____

_____

_____

_____

DIG DEEPER

The story of Israel's journey from captivity to the land of promise is filled with both miracles and missteps. On the stage of history, God has given us pictures of our own lives individually and of His big-picture redemption for the human race. The images of Passover, a parted sea, day-by-day provision, a covenant of love and commitment, trials and temptations, failures and successes, and a long and winding road continue to resonate deep in our hearts. We can relate both positively and negatively to Moses, to Israel's slaves, to Joshua and Caleb, to the negative spies, to the complaining wanderers, and to the faithful who persist in the long journey. The story of salvation is comprehensive. It is a historical fact, a present process, and a future promise. It's not only something that happens in a moment, it's also a lifelong reality. It's not only Israel's experience, but our story as well!

MOSES AND PHARAOH

Read Exodus 2:23–3:15. What does God's perspective on His people's condition show us about His heart? What is His purpose for them? What does Moses' response tell us about him?

Read Exodus 6:1-9. What stands out to you about God's announced intentions? Look at verse 9. Note the people's response. Can you relate? Are there divine promises that, given your current situation, seem too good to believe? Share an instance when you've struggled to hope for good things because you're surrounded by bad things.

PASSOVER AND THE RED SEA

Read Exodus 12:21-28. Why do you think God chose to deliver Israel from Egypt in such a visually symbolic way? How do you think these people were impacted by having to kill a lamb and splash its blood around their door frames? What was the lesson for the Israelites? For us?

God, via a cloud by day and a column of fire by night, led Moses and the people to the edge of the Red Sea—a place of extreme vulnerability. They seemed completely trapped between a huge body of water and an intimidating army. Why do you think God didn't lead them straight out of Egypt and into the Promised Land? In what areas of your life—spiritually, relationally, or in your circumstances— have you felt yourself to be boxed in or trapped? What does this event say about God's ways with His people?

GLORY, COVENANT, AND PRESENCE

The first of the Ten Commandments is, "You shall have no other gods before me" (Exodus 20:3). Why do you think this commandment comes first? What relevance do you think the Ten Commandments have for us today?

At Mount Sinai, God demonstrated His power with lightning, thunder, smoke, a loud blast, and other awe-inspiring manifestations. Yet in Exodus 33:18, Moses asked to see God's glory. Why do you think Moses thought he had not seen God's glory yet? Of all the ways God described Himself in Exodus 34:5 when passing in front of Moses, which one is most meaningful to you? Why?

Read Exodus 40:34-38 and 29:43-46. What does it say to you that the God of the universe wanted to designate a place where His people could meet with Him? Where are the modern-day people of God supposed to meet with Him?

12 SPIES

Read Numbers 13:30–14:11, then read Hebrews 3:7-12. How would you have reacted to the situation if you had been one of the spies exploring the land? All the spies saw the same thing; what enabled Caleb and Joshua to interpret the situation differently? What words did God and the writer of Hebrews use to characterize the response of the 10 spies?

THE WILDERNESS EXPERIENCE

Many Israelites complained about the journey to the Promised Land and wanted to go back to the ease and fruitfulness of Egypt—forgetting both the pain of their slavery in the past and the promised blessings of their future. In what ways do we tend to do the same thing? How does focusing on God's promises help us with adversity? with temptation? with contentment? with the battle between faith and unbelief?

In what ways does God provide for us day by day in "desert" situations?

Promised Land

PROMISED LAND
Joshua
Judges
Ruth

BEGINNINGS
Genesis

WANDERINGS
Exodus
Leviticus
Numbers
Deuteronomy

DIVIDED KINGDOM

2 Kings 12-25
2 Chronicles 10-36
Isaiah
Jeremiah
Lamentations
Hosea
Joel
Amos
Obadiah
Jonah
Micah
Nahum
Habakkuk
Zephaniah

UNITED KINGDOM

1 & 2 Samuel
1 Kings 1-11
1 Chronicles
2 Chronicles 1-9
Psalms
Proverbs
Ecclesiastes
Song of Songs

CAPTIVITY & THE COMING KINGDOM

Ezra
Nehemiah
Esther
Ezekiel
Daniel
Haggai
Zechariah
Malachi

Joshua, the Jordan, and Jericho

Joshua 1-6

Read Joshua 1:1-9; 4:1-14; 5:13–6:21

"Be strong and very courageous. Be careful to obey all the law my servant Moses gave you; do not turn from it to the right or to the left, that you may be successful wherever you go." (Joshua 1:7 NIV)

Joshua was in an unenviable position: How do you follow an act like Moses? Moses had spent long hours speaking face to face with God, so much so, that for a while he literally glowed with the radiant glory of God! Through Moses, God did one miracle after another. And when the people questioned Moses' leadership, God dealt with them harshly. Now Moses was gone, and the burden of leadership was on Joshua. In addition, that land of promise—the one filled with "giants" and fortified cities, according to the spies—spread overwhelmingly in front of him. There were enormous expectations and enormous obstacles. Joshua surely struggled internally with all this, prompting God to remind him repeatedly not to be afraid. "I am with you" God assured him. His primary tasks were to follow God and do all that Moses had commanded. Then all would be well.

Scouts were again sent into the land, and they received assistance from Rahab, a prostitute in Jericho who was able to recognize what God was doing. Because of her faith, she and her household would be spared. Led by priests carrying the ark of the covenant, the nation crossed through the parted waters of the Jordan River. Before they could engage in war, they first had to be "consecrated"—set apart as God's unique people. This generation had not been marked with circumcision, the sign of the covenant. So at Gilgal, they prepared themselves spiritually for the physical battles that would come. A divine figure, the commander of the Lord's armies, appeared to Joshua to signify God's promised presence.

The conquest of Canaan began at Jericho. And what peculiar battle instructions! God commanded His people to march around the fortified city for seven days. They did, and when they shouted and sounded their trumpets, the walls fell and God's people took the city. The first victory in the Promised Land had been won. God had taken His people through a long, arduous, disorienting process, full of twists, missteps, and delays, and brought them miraculously into His promise.

REFLECTION

- What situations in your life are calling for you to be strong and courageous and to know that God will never leave you? How do Joshua's situation and God's assurances encourage you?
- Why would God choose difficult situations (i.e., a river at flood stage, a thick-walled city) and unusual commands (i.e., silently marching around a city for seven days) to accomplish His purposes?

- What "Promised Land"—a calling, an assignment, a vision—has God given you? How does Israel's path of trust, obedience, consecration, and action relate to you?

NOTES/JOURNAL

_____

_____

_____

_____

_____

_____

_____

_____

_____

_____

_____

_____

_____

_____

_____

_____

_____

BOTTOM LINE
God is fully able to get us into the places He has called us, and He will never leave us or forsake us in the process.

PRAY for the grace to remember God's presence with you and for the courage to boldly go and do the things He has called you to do.

Conquest of the Land

Joshua 7-24

Read Joshua 14:6-15; 23; 24:11-28

"Choose for yourselves this day whom you will serve, whether the gods your ancestors served beyond the Euphrates, or the gods of the Amorites, in whose land you are living. But as for me and my household, we will serve the LORD."
(Joshua 24:15 NIV)

Compared to the great city of Jericho, Ai looked like a country village. Conquering it would be a piece of (manna) cake. Or so Israel thought. Military "experts" suggested sending only part of the army. But the battle resulted in an embarrassing defeat. Why? God has required all the spoils from Jericho—perhaps an offering of the first and best of the Promised Land—yet someone had kept a few things for himself. One man's greed defiled the entire nation and prompted God to remove His favor until they dealt with the treachery. Once they did, victories came again.

Having discovered the consequences of corruption, Israel next faced the consequences of compromise. Local kings pretended to be distant, and foreign kings proposed a peace treaty with Joshua. Rather than ask the Lord, Israel's leaders used their own judgment and ended up with an unbreakable pact with local inhabitants who would remain in the land for centuries to come.

In a fierce battle in defense of these new allies, Joshua commanded the sun and moon to stand still, and God extended a day. Enemies were defeated, and the conquest continued with a divide-and-conquer strategy: first, southern Canaan, then the territory to the north. Pockets of the Promised Land would remain unconquered, but most of it was divided among the tribes. Caleb, the last of his generation still living besides Joshua, finally received his portion of the promise. And the Levites, the tribe of priests, were given a holy assignment rather than land. In his old age and parting words, Joshua reminded Israel of God's faithfulness to them—not one word of His promise had failed (23:14). He insisted they reaffirm their allegiance to God. If they wanted to serve the Lord, they would have to forsake all their lingering idols. In a solemn ceremony, they pledged themselves to the Lord. This renewal of Israel's covenant with God is the backdrop for the era of the Judges.

REFLECTION

- What kinds of obstacles and temptations did Joshua and his people face? In what ways can this book of Israel's battles serve as a manual for how we should face the challenges and adversity in our own lives?
- Joshua challenged the nation of Israel to choose whom they would serve. In what ways is this a choice we have to make every day? Can you give some practical, real-life examples of how this choice gets played out at home or at work?

• What was Israel's experience with God's promises? What part did they play in their fulfillment? What part did God play? What lessons or what applications can you glean from Israel's experience as you to try to cling to God's promises?

NOTES/JOURNAL

_____

_____

_____

_____

_____

_____

_____

_____

_____

_____

_____

_____

_____

_____

_____

_____

_____

_____

_____

BOTTOM LINE
God fulfills His Word to those who accept it and follow it faithfully, becoming their defender, provider, deliverer, warrior, and more.

PRAY for God to show you any "idols" in your life (i.e., any people or things or gods, etc., that you value more than you value Him). Ask Him to help you deepen your commitment to Him.

The Judges Cycle
Judges

Read Judges 2:6-23

"In those days Israel had no king; all the people did whatever seemed right in their own eyes." (Judges 21:25 NLT)

Imagine a culture where the only rule is: "Do whatever you feel is best, whatever seems best to you." Can you imagine the chaos? All those colliding desires and competing wills? Talk about a recipe for anarchy!

Sadly, in the time of the judges, when Israel did not yet have a king, this was life in the Promised Land. The nation—really more like a loose confederation of tribes—went through a really dark period. Over and over, like a bad déjà vu dream, the people sinned against God, suffered the discipline of God (in the form of oppression from their godless neighbors), cried out to God for help, and then experienced rescue by God (through a deliverer or "judge"). As a nation, Israel seemed to suffer from amnesia. They forgot both who they were and whose they were. Like an unfaithful spouse, they gave their affections to other gods.

Not coincidentally, this was also perhaps the most brutal and depraved era in Israel's history. Lawlessness prompted vigilante justice, which escalated into open warfare. The worst such episode was the tribal war between the tribe of Benjamin and the other 11 tribes, provoked by a violent rape in one of the towns in Benjamite territory. About 25,000 of Benjamin's warriors were massacred in the ensuing battles, and the tribe was temporarily cut off from the nation. Only later did the other tribes allow Benjamite men to marry outside their own tribe, and the population was slowly replenished. This state of semi-anarchy would set the stage for the confederation to become a kingdom.

In retrospect, we know that God's ultimate solution for the human condition is not more laws. But neither is it lawlessness. And until the inner nature of human beings is transformed, humanity will swing wildly between those two extremes. Judges shows us the unfortunate outcome of lawlessness. The commitment made at the end of the book of Joshua to forsake other gods and serve God alone had long been forgotten. And the need for a lasting divine solution was becoming more clear.

REFLECTION
- Imagine in your town if the only rule were, "Do whatever feels right to you." What would daily life be like?
- What big commitments have you made to God in your life and when? In what ways and what circumstances do these commitments tend to slip from our memories? What can we do practically, specifically, daily, to keep from forgetting?
- What forms of idolatry do you think tempt us most in modern society? Which ones are your greatest temptations?

NOTES/JOURNAL

_____

_____

_____

_____

_____

_____

_____

_____

_____

_____

_____

_____

_____

_____

_____

_____

_____

_____

_____

BOTTOM LINE

Sin leads to oppression and enslavement, and only God can set us free.

PRAY for God to help you (and your loved ones) break free from any cycles of sin. Ask God to bring about a spiritual awakening in our culture.

Deborah, Gideon, and Samson

Judges 4-8, 13-16

Read Judges 6:1-16; 16:4-31

"If the Lord is with us, why has all this happened to us? And where are all the miracles our ancestors told us about?" . . . Then the Lord turned to him and said, "Go with the strength you have, and rescue Israel from the Midianites. I am sending you!"
(Judges 6:13-14 NLT)

Oftentimes—not always*—when God seems far away, it's because we—not He—moved. We are, as the old hymn says, "prone to wander." This was certainly the case for Israel during the time of the judges.

One of those judges, a timid man named Gideon, asked his divine visitor why his people were suffering such oppression. He also inquired about the absence of divine miracles in his day. The Lord might have responded, "I said this is what would happen if you worshiped other gods." Instead, God simply sent this tentative, anxious "warrior" on a mission to help his fellow Israelites break free from the power of the Midianites. And He would accomplish it by reducing Gideon's army from an impressive 32,000 to a mere 300 men and giving them a creative tactic to cause the enemy to defeat itself.

That divine strategy isn't unlike the victory God had earlier given Deborah. She had numerous warriors at her disposal too, but the stroke that freed Israel from Canaanite oppression came from a bold housewife named Jael who took advantage of an opportunity to kill the Canaanite general while he slept.

Much later, God opposed the Philistines' oppression of His people not through an army but through a man named Samson, who had been dedicated to God from birth. Samson was physically strong and morally weak. The Nazirite vow his parents had taken on his behalf meant never cutting his hair. It was in the keeping of that vow that his strength was found. When Samson mentioned this fact to his Philistine lover Delilah, she betrayed him. With his hair cut and his eyes gouged out, he became a slave to the Philistines. Only when his hair grew back did he inflict one last devastating blow on the enemy and free Israel from oppression.

These deliverers were far from perfect, but they were divinely appointed and empowered. And that divine calling and enablement was why they succeeded even in their weakness. Every time, Israel deserved their captivity; but every time, their cries reached God's ears. He let them experience the consequences of their sin, but He never disowned them as His chosen nation. He is faithful even when His people are not.

*Sometimes God "hides Himself" so that our faith might become stronger, so that we might learn to trust in what we can't see or "feel."

REFLECTION

• Why do you think God chose to work through Gideon in spite of his fear, and through Samson in spite of his flaws?

- Why is it significant that in a culture dominated by men, God chose Deborah to liberate His people?
- Have you ever felt unqualified to serve God? If so, why? In what ways do the stories of Deborah, Gideon, Samson, and the other judges address those feelings?

NOTES/JOURNAL

_____

_____

_____

_____

_____

_____

_____

_____

_____

_____

_____

_____

_____

_____

_____

_____

_____

_____

_____

BOTTOM LINE
God uses imperfect people to accomplish His purposes.

PRAY for God to work in and through you and through government leaders. Ask God to encourage someone who thinks he/she is useless to God.

Ruth

Ruth 1-4

Read Ruth 1, 3:1-13

"Wherever you go, I will go, and wherever you live, I will live; your people will be my people, and your God will be my God." (Ruth 1:16 HCSB)

During the time of the judges, one family moved to neighboring Moab because of a famine—one of the consequences of idolatry and disobedience, as God had foretold through Moses and Joshua. Perhaps this family didn't realize what a significant statement they were making by leaving the Promised Land for a rival territory. Or perhaps they knew the sinfulness of the people well enough to know the famine might last for a while. Regardless, their time in Moab did not go well. The husband and the two sons died, leaving a bitter widow/mother and her two widowed daughters-in-law, both Moabites. When this widow, Naomi, heard things were better back in Bethlehem, she returned home with one of her widowed daughters-in-law, Ruth, who insisted on leaving her homeland and adopting the people of Israel as her own.

The result is a beautiful love story with profound symbolism: God not only redeems His people but also those who join with His people. Ruth was one of the few during the dark time of the judges who did not merely do what seemed right in her own eyes. She was a selfless, honest, diligent worker who stood out to Boaz (a distant relative of hers via her dead husband). Naomi devised a plan for Ruth to suggest to Boaz that he follow an old Hebrew custom/expectation and "redeem" her (that is, marry her and give her descendants). Boaz agreed, covering her with his garments which was an ancient way of symbolizing his intent to protect and provide for her. The two married and had a son named Obed. He eventually become the grandfather of David, Israel's greatest king.

The story of Ruth beautifully demonstrates blessing in a time of want, truth in a time of chaos, and redemption in a time of futility. Naomi's bitterness was undone, Ruth's desire to be part of Israel's family was fulfilled, and their descendants would impact God's kingdom forever. This family's story is also ours: desperate need and suffering met by God's kindness and restoration, with a plentiful harvest as the backdrop. Those who return to God's promise and hope in Him will eventually experience His blessing in full.

REFLECTION

- Why is the book of Ruth more than a nice love story? In what ways does the story represent the human condition and God's response to it? In what ways does it reflect the story of your life?
- Have past traumas, broken relationships, or adverse circumstances created bitterness in you? If so, how does the story of Ruth encourage you? What does it tell us about God's compassion for our hardships?
- What desires are stirred up in you by the story of Naomi, Ruth, and Boaz? Why? How can you expect God to fulfill those desires?

NOTES/JOURNAL

_____
_____
_____
_____
_____
_____
_____
_____
_____
_____
_____
_____
_____
_____
_____
_____
_____
_____
_____
_____

BOTTOM LINE

God is a redeemer and restorer. He heals wounds, restores blessings, comforts those who grieve, and gives us new starts and a lasting legacy.

PRAY that God would show you any pockets of bitterness in your heart and that you'd cling to Him through times of uncertainty and/or grief.

Jesus in the Promised Land

The pictures of Jesus in Joshua, Judges, and Ruth are perhaps less noticeable than in other portions of Scripture, but they are just as profound. He is behind the scenes in . . .

1. Joshua. Joshua and Jesus are essentially the same name—"God is salvation"—and both are appointed by God to lead us into the Promised Land.
2. Rahab's scarlet cord. The prostitute who hosted and helped Israel's spies in Jericho was given a symbol that would notify Israel's army to save her and her family from destruction. The scarlet cord hung out of her window in the wall of the city hints at the blood of Jesus that saves us from destruction.
3. The commander of the Lord's army. The divine visitor who came to Joshua before the battle of Jericho in Joshua 5 is not named. Is it an angel? Perhaps, but the fact that he told Joshua to remove his sandals on holy ground and allowed Joshua to bow to him suggests that he may have been the preincarnate Christ.
4. Judges. The judges themselves offer faint pictures of Jesus, but other than that, He's hard to find in this book. But that's the point. The people were in desperate need of a Savior, and none of their deliverers were sufficient for more than a brief moment in time. The entire book cries out for a divine rescuer.
5. Ruth. The distant relative Boaz redeems the Gentile Ruth, who aligned herself with God's people and purposes. She who was once alienated from the people of God was grafted into them, covered by the protective garments of the redeemer.

NOTES/JOURNAL

_____

_____

_____

_____

_____

_____

_____

_____

_____

_____

_____

_____

_____

_____

_____

_____

_____

_____

_____

_____

_____

_____

_____

_____

_____

LOOK AHEAD

What is the solution for a society in which everyone does what is right in his own eyes? God wanted to be their king Himself, but they kept turning their eyes from Him and going their own way. This nation longs for the structure God has already given them, but eventually the anarchy of their culture will prompt them to cry out for a human king, and God will grant them their desire. But first, God will give them a trustworthy spiritual leader to address corrupt worship practices.

OVERVIEW

At last God is leading His people into the Promised Land! Though it is sheer gift, the nation of Israel also has to act. This new generation must have the courage to grasp what God has promised. When they do they will face the intimidating inhabitants and fortified cities seen by their parents and grandparents some 40 years earlier. God has guaranteed success, but only if His people move forward in faith, not retreat in fear. For this reason, God repeatedly tells Joshua (Moses' replacement) to be strong and courageous.

In the book of Joshua, the Israelites take most of the God-given territory of Canaan, but not without a few setbacks and some hard lessons learned. In the book of Judges, a low point in Israel's history, the people foolishly repeat a cycle of sinning against God, suffering the discipline of God, crying out to God, and being delivered by God. The events of the book of Ruth (set during this grim period of the Judges) serve as an encouraging reminder that not everyone was guilty of doing "what was right in his own eyes" (Judges 21:25 NASB). A few remained faithful.

THE STORY: LIFE IN THE PROMISED LAND

At the beginning of the book of **Joshua**, the people are poised to cross the Jordan River and enter the Promised Land. But Moses has died, and Joshua is having to rise to the moment. So is the new generation; none of them has military training. They've spent the last 40 years wandering around the wilderness, burying their parents, not fighting. They are reminded not to fear and to remember everything God has told them. This entire generation needs to be circumcised and set apart. But when the time comes, the waters of the Jordan part, the people enter the land, and the conquest begins.

Jericho's walls fall in miraculous fashion, but subsequent battles don't always go that smoothly. Some of the Israelites give in to temptation and disobey divine instructions. Others make compromises. In those instances, the result is less success in battle and more obstacles to overcome. In time the land is largely, though not completely, conquered. Next it is divided among the 12 tribes. Caleb and Joshua finally receive what they trusted God could accomplish four decades earlier. The next era of Israel's history, covered by the book of **Judges**, is a time of semi-lawlessness. Imagine the spirit of the Old West set in ancient Israel and you get the picture. Many Israelites forget God's faithfulness and become enamored with the gods of the people they have just conquered. When they begin to suffer the consequences of their disobedience, they cry out to God and He raises up a deliverer (or "judge") to come to their rescue. Soon after relief comes, however, the cycle begins again. Among the many "judges" from this period are Deborah, Gideon, and Samson. At one point, the nation even experiences civil war: the tribe of Benjamin facing off against the other eleven tribes. We grimace at all this "mess," wondering if God's chosen people might actually forfeit their calling. But even in the midst of chaos, God gives hopeful glimpses of restoration. One of those signs is the amazing story of **Ruth**, which tells of a devastated Jewish family in Moab. Brought back to the Promised Land and to a place of abundance, Ruth and her mother-in-law experience God's favor and blessing. They set the stage for Israel's most glorious era.

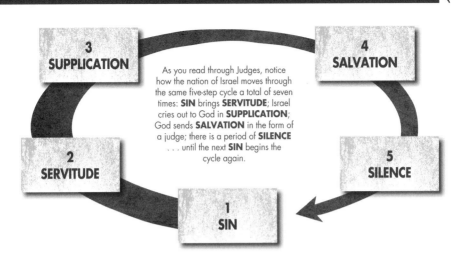

As you read through Judges, notice how the nation of Israel moves through the same five-step cycle a total of seven times: **SIN** brings **SERVITUDE**; Israel cries out to God in **SUPPLICATION**; God sends **SALVATION** in the form of a judge; there is a period of **SILENCE** . . . until the next **SIN** begins the cycle again.

3 **SUPPLICATION**

4 **SALVATION**

2 **SERVITUDE**

5 **SILENCE**

1 **SIN**

WATCH

The period of the judges puts the worst of human nature on display, even in the midst of God's good promises and provision. As you watch the video, think about the ways your human nature has conflicted with His purposes for your life. How have you repeated bad patterns? What has God done to meet you in your time and place of need? How is He restoring you to wholeness and fulfilling your purpose?

VIDEO NOTES

VIDEO REFLECTION/GROUP DISCUSSION

What makes it so attractive to follow the crowd?

DIG DEEPER

The people who were supposed to be different from all other peoples became an awful lot like the nations around them. At times, due to disobedience, they even came under the control of those nations! We face a similar challenge. For a long time now, Christians have been debating the question: How integrated into or separated from the larger culture should we be? The Bible says we are to be in the world without being of the world, but what exactly does that look like in day-to-day life? Do we build, maintain, and remain in a separate, distinct, Christian subculture? Or do we purposely move about within secular culture in order to share the gospel and have an eternal impact? In short, how do we influence our culture for Christ without embracing worldly values? This is a difficult line to navigate, and granted, our calling as the Church is a bit different than Israel's calling prior to 1000 B.C. But we can surely relate to the natural human tendency to compromise and conform. As you study Israel's conquest of the Promised Land and the subsequent time of the Judges, pay attention to what the ancient people of God did right … and wrong.

JOSHUA, THE JORDAN, AND JERICHO

Read Joshua 1:7-9. What are the benefits of this promise? What are the conditions? How would you apply these verses, which were originally about entering a physical Promised Land, to our lives today?

Joshua 3:15 says that the Jordan was at flood stage when it was time for Israel to cross it. Why do you think God chose those virtually impossible conditions? What does this tell us about His ways? How and where have you seen Him do this in your life?

In order to conquer Jericho, the people had to march around the city for days and shout the last time around. How would you have felt if God gave you instructions like this? Would you have seen the wisdom in following them? Why or why not?

CONQUEST OF THE LAND

When the people were faithful to God, they had great victories in their battles. When they were not faithful—or even when only one or two of them were not faithful—they often experienced defeat. Is it fair for God to do this—to cause an entire people to suffer for the actions of a few? Why or why not?

Read Joshua 14:6-15. What does this story say about God's faithfulness? How does it challenge our assumptions about aging and the "prime of life"? What do you think Caleb might say about our modern notion of retirement?

THE JUDGES CYCLE

Describe the "Judges Cycle" (that occurs seven times in the book). How does this play out in your own life? Do you tend to cry out to God only when you're in trouble? What are the dangers of this pattern? What benefits and blessings are we missing when we relate to Him this way?

DEBORAH, GIDEON, AND SAMSON

There were many judges in Israel in this era, but three of the most prominent—Deborah, Gideon, and Samson—were also the most surprising. Deborah was a woman, Gideon was fearful, and Samson had moral weaknesses. Why do you think God chose them to be leaders? What does this tell us about God's ways? How does this relate to our expectations for the people He chooses? Which one of these would you have had the hardest time following?

RUTH

Read Ruth 1:16-17. Considering Ruth's background as a Moabite (a Gentile from a nation at times hostile toward Israel), why is this a surprising statement? What longings are represented in this plea? Where have you seen this kind of fierce commitment?

The book of Ruth begins in bitterness and ends with deep contentment. In what ways is this a picture of God's purposes? What can we do to position ourselves for this kind of experience with God?

United Kingdom

BEGINNINGS

Genesis

PROMISED LAND

Joshua
Judges
Ruth

WANDERINGS

Exodus
Leviticus
Numbers
Deuteronomy

Divided Kingdom

2 Kings 12-25
2 Chronicles 10-36
Isaiah
Jeremiah
Lamentations
Hosea
Joel
Amos
Obadiah
Jonah
Micah
Nahum
Habakkuk
Zephaniah

Captivity & the Coming Kingdom

Ezra
Nehemiah
Esther
Ezekiel
Daniel
Haggai
Zechariah
Malachi

United Kingdom

1 & 2 Samuel
1 Kings 1-11
1 Chronicles
2 Chronicles 1-9
Psalms
Proverbs
Ecclesiastes
Song of Songs

Samuel

1 Samuel 1-12

Read 1 Samuel 3; 8:4-22

"I asked the Lord to give me this boy, and he has granted my request. Now I am giving
him to the Lord, and he will belong to the Lord his whole life."
(1 Samuel 1:27-28 NLT)

Hannah prayed a desperate prayer, asking God to give her a son. In return, she promised to dedicate him completely to God. Hannah's desire was God's opportunity to turn the nation from its corruption. The tiny answer to prayer would grow to become a prophet. He would replace Israel's existing spiritual leaders who were abusing their priestly privileges. He would lead the nation through times of oppression at the hands of the neighboring Philistines.

Samuel was that baby boy. Hannah placed him under the training and service of the priest Eli, and as a youngster he heard God's call (which in those days was rare, apparently due to the nation's spiritual indifference). It took three times before Samuel realized the identity of the one speaking, but God soon gave him a message of judgment against Eli's family and the nation as a whole. Sure enough, the corrupt priestly family was wiped out and the Philistines captured the ark of the covenant (though they were traumatized by God's holy presence, and would soon send the ark back, along with some gifts). The prophet Samuel seized upon these events to call the people to repent of their idolatry as the path to freedom from Philistine oppression. He then led them into a purer practice of worship and relationship with God.

When the people demanded a king, Samuel was offended, but he went to God with the request. God had him clearly explain the costs and benefits of having a human ruler, and then he was to anoint Saul as the nation's first king. God sovereignly fulfilled His purposes through their request, even though the request was unfortunate. Samuel would later voice prophetic judgment against Saul and anoint David as Israel's future king. In his farewell address, Samuel echoed the words of Moses and Joshua centuries earlier: worship God alone and enjoy His blessings, or forsake Him and suffer living without Him. The nation formerly described as a place where everyone did whatever was right in their own eyes began the journey back to doing what was right in God's eyes.

REFLECTION

- How did Hannah's prayer for herself intersect with God's purposes? How can we ensure that our prayers align with God's purposes?
- In Scripture, do you see a relationship between vibrant worship of God and the welfare of God's people? Do you think any such relationship applies to you? Why or why not?
- In 1 Samuel 12:23, Samuel suggests that it would be sinful not to pray for God's people. Do you think that's true only for someone in his role as a spiritual leader or for everyone in God's kingdom? To what degree are we responsible to pray for others? for our own community and nation? for other nations?

NOTES/JOURNAL

_____

_____

_____

_____

_____

_____

_____

_____

_____

_____

_____

_____

_____

_____

_____

_____

_____

_____

_____

BOTTOM LINE

When God's people cry out to Him, God is faithful to meet their needs and to fulfill His purposes.

PRAY that God would fulfill His purposes in your life (and the lives of those you love) in ways that far exceed your wildest dreams.

King Saul

1 Samuel 13-15; 1 Chronicles 9:35–10:14

Read 1 Samuel 10:17-27; 13:5-15; 15:10-23

"What is more pleasing to the LORD: your burnt offerings and sacrifices or your obedience to his voice?" (1 Samuel 15:22 NLT)

King Saul began well. He demonstrated decisive leadership on behalf of the people and against Israel's enemies. He and his son, Jonathan, fought effective battles against the nation's oppressors and instilled a renewed confidence in Israel's army. Yet from the early years of his kingship, he showed signs of rash behavior, specifically a vow that, if carried out, would have resulted in Jonathan's death. It was this impulsive streak that triggered the incident that disqualified Saul from the throne. While waiting to do battle with the Philistines and nervously watching Israel's troops scatter, he wrongfully assumed the role of the priest. He offered the sacrifice that Samuel was supposed to offer. Upon his arrival, Samuel confronted Saul and spoke God's message of rejection, "Now your kingdom must end" (1 Samuel 13:14 NLT).

Not long afterward, Saul disobeyed again and received another divine rebuke. God told him to completely destroy the people who had first opposed Israel after the Exodus, the Amalekites—people, livestock, everything. But Saul carried out the instructions only to a point. When Samuel confronted him, Saul gave spiritual-sounding excuses, but neither Samuel nor God was moved. What followed was a gut-wrenching plea to retain his kingship, and a firm denial of the request. Saul and Samuel would never see each other again.

Soon Saul's reign—and his sanity—began to disintegrate. A young harpist named David played soothing music to calm him, but that relationship soon disintegrated too. The king Israel had begged for and who began so well proved to be a disaster. And God regretted ever choosing him in the first place. Saul had a heart for the throne but not a heart for God.

REFLECTION

- Why do you think God was angry with Saul for an impatient sacrifice before battle and an attempt to do just enough to fulfill an assignment? Why is it not enough to do most of what God says when He gives specific instructions? What does this reflect about the condition of a heart?
- In what ways have you been tempted recently to compromise with God? What priorities might you have placed above doing what He says is right?
- Why do you think God didn't give Saul another chance?

NOTES/JOURNAL

_____

_____

_____

_____

_____

_____

_____

_____

_____

_____

_____

_____

_____

_____

_____

_____

_____

_____

_____

_____

BOTTOM LINE

Cutting corners in a relationship with God can result in disappointment and regret—and a loss of God-given opportunities.

PRAY for purity of heart—for God to show you any areas of life where you are lacking in integrity.

Saul vs. David

1 Samuel 16-31

Read 1 Samuel 16:1-13; 18:6-16

*Taste and see that the Lord is good; blessed is the one who takes refuge in him.
. . . The righteous cry out, and the Lord hears them; he delivers them from all their
troubles. (Psalm 34:8, 17 NIV)*

After rejecting Saul, God sent Samuel to the family of Jesse to secretly anoint the next king. Jesse didn't even call the youngest son, David, to the event—he was apparently out of favor with his brothers and seemingly too inexperienced to be king. Yet David was God's surprising choice. God selected him because God looks at the heart. This young ruler would not be made in the mold of Saul!

Saul didn't know his replacement had already been anointed, so he had no reason not to like David. After all, David had boldly defeated the mocking Philistine giant Goliath in battle. What's more, David played the harp beautifully, often soothing Saul's tormented soul. But when David's popularity began to grow beyond Saul's, a raging jealousy began to devour Saul. Soon David was on the run, hiding in caves and even pretending to be crazy, all in an effort to avoid the paranoid, murderous Saul. A ragtag band of marginalized but fierce warriors joined with David, and together they survived for years.

In the deserts of Judah, David actually had two chances to kill Saul, but he let them pass. On both occasions, David collected evidence that he had been close enough to harm Saul. Then he called out to the king from a distance to try to convince Saul that he had no intention to hurt him. David's respect for the Lord's anointed was too great for him to try to manipulate circumstances for his own good. He believed God would put him on the throne in God's perfect time. When Saul and his sons died in battle, David grieved. But the wait for the throne was over.

Wilderness experiences seem to teach a lot of lessons. That was true after the Exodus, and it's true in David's life. He learned patience, persistence, restraint, faith, and how to overcome fear and anxiety, among other things. And he wrote about his experiences. Many of his psalms were prayers. Yet these psalms invariably end in worship and gratitude because David trusted God's faithfulness. David's wilderness years were anything but easy, but that dark time was the perfect training for a future king who would rule with wholehearted passion for God and His purposes.

REFLECTION

- Have you experienced a calling or promise from God that has taken years to unfold? How have you responded to the challenges and delays? How does David's experience encourage you?
- Why do you think David experienced such fierce and relentless opposition to his calling? In what ways have you experienced opposition to God's plans for you?

- What does it mean to "take refuge in the Lord"? How can you apply this to your circumstances and relationships?

NOTES/JOURNAL

_____

_____

_____

_____

_____

_____

_____

_____

_____

_____

_____

_____

_____

_____

_____

_____

_____

_____

BOTTOM LINE
The path to God's purposes and promises isn't short or easy, but it is certain for those who persevere in faith and obedience.

PRAY for perseverance in faith, and obedience and willingness to be conformed to Christ.

DAY 4

King David

2 Samuel; 1 Chronicles 11-29; Psalms

Read 2 Samuel 7:1-17; 12:1-15; 1 Chronicles 28

*"I have asked one thing from the L*ORD*; it is what I desire: to dwell in the house of the L*ORD *all the days of my life, gazing on the beauty of the L*ORD *and seeking Him in His temple." (Psalm 27:4 HCSB)*

David was a worshiper at heart. He insisted on bringing the ark of the covenant to Jerusalem. He determined to honor God in all the nation's activities. Most of all, he dreamed of building a worship center in Jerusalem that would be filled with priests and musicians offering round-the-clock offerings and praise to God. This beautiful temple would house the ark, feature altars for sacrifice, and provide a gathering place for the nation's worshipers at feast times. David made the presence and praise of God the top priority.

David accomplished plenty of other things during his reign. He captured Jebus and made it the capital, Jerusalem. He consolidated the loosely organized tribes under one united kingdom. And he won decisive battles over the Philistines. But he never got to build the temple. God promised it would happen, but not in David's lifetime. Instead, God promised to establish David's throne forever and give him rest from his enemies. David would be allowed to draw up blueprints for the temple, plan its dedication, write psalms about it, collect money for it, and everything else necessary to set it up. But his son Solomon would be given the privilege of building it.

Sadly, David is also well-known for his adulterous affair with Bathsheba, and his murderous cover-up. From that point forward, his household was tumultuous. He faced rebellion (once from his own son), warfare with other nations, the death of several sons, and harsh divine discipline for taking an unauthorized census. He was by no means perfect, but he knew how to repent with all his heart and persevere with all his strength. In the end, he gave thanks. God had shown him favor, his legacy would last, and the united kingdom would be left in the hands of a capable and wise son. The man after God's own heart had lived with passion and purpose, holding nothing back. And God honored his efforts, forgave his sins, and gave him lasting promises that would shape God's kingdom forever.

REFLECTION

- What would your life look like if you could fully live with passion and purpose, holding nothing back? In what ways did this approach to life benefit David and the people around him? In what ways did it cause trouble for him and those around him?
- Why do you think God was so harsh toward Saul's sins and so forgiving toward David's?
- Do you have a single, great desire for God's kingdom like David did? If so, what is it? If not, how do you think God would respond if you prayed for one?

NOTES/JOURNAL

_____

_____

_____

_____

_____

_____

_____

_____

_____

_____

_____

_____

_____

_____

_____

_____

_____

_____

_____

_____

BOTTOM LINE

God loves passionate worship and favors those who live wholeheartedly toward Him.

PRAY for passion in your worship of God, and for His glory in your life and in the lives of your children.

King Solomon

1 Kings 1-11; 2 Chronicles 1-9; Proverbs; Song of Songs; Ecclesiastes

Read 1 Kings 3:1-15; 2 Chronicles 5; 1 Kings 11:1-13

Above all else, guard your heart, for everything you do flows from it. (Proverbs 4:23)

When offered "a blank check" from God, Solomon asked for wisdom. God gave it to him in spades. God also gave him extravagant wealth, fame, and success. He would become the richest and wisest king on earth, and kings and queens from other nations would marvel at the glory of Solomon's accomplishments. Among those accomplishments were the temple that his father David longed to build and a palace worthy of a wise and wealthy king. He also built up Israel's army (but with Egyptian horses and weapons, against God's law); he built up Israel's labor force (but by requiring difficult labor that strained his people); and accumulated an enormous harem of women (but by marrying foreign wives, often to create foreign alliances, against God's law). His accomplishments were great, but the means to those ends were costly and questionable. Solomon had a heart for God's kingdom, but also a heart for making moral and ethical compromises to build it. In other words, he had a divided heart.

Perhaps that's why Solomon ultimately was not satisfied with all his wealth, fame, and success. The king whose name means "peace" (*shalom*) had peace on every side, but he was not at peace within. He loved God plus a whole lot of other things, which can never lead to complete contentment. He penned beautiful expressions of wisdom but failed to live up to many of them. The king who urged his sons to seek wisdom above all else and guard their hearts somehow forgot to guard his own. By the end of his life, he had been seduced not only by foreign women but also by their gods, and he even supported their false worship. The nation that had been called to worship God alone was about to slip back into gross forms of idolatry, largely because their king was modeling this kind of disobedience.

That's why a limited love for God and partial obedience isn't really true love for God or obedience at all. Solomon's words in Ecclesiastes reflect the disillusionment of someone who had everything, but realized he had nothing because God wasn't at the center of it. The kingdom of Israel expanded and flourished under his reign—for a time—but it would soon wither and divide. For centuries, the Jews would long for the former glory of a kingdom whose king gained, and lost, nearly everything.

REFLECTION
- Why do you think Solomon did not end his life or his reign well? How can we avoid the same discontentment?
- What do you think is involved in guarding your heart? According to Proverbs 4:23, why is this so important?
- Based on lessons from Solomon's life, what attitudes honor God? What attitudes alienate us from Him? Does the New Testament truth of being "in Christ" change this dynamic? Why or why not?

NOTES/JOURNAL

BOTTOM LINE
God's blessings are available to all who ask but are enjoyed only by those who steward them well.

PRAY for spiritual awareness: to God's presence, to temptation, to opportunities to serve God.

DAY 6-7 Jesus in the United Kingdom

In a portion of Scripture that gives us glimpses of the coming kingdom, it should be no surprise that there are also glimpses of the coming King. In the united kingdom, Jesus is behind the scenes in . . .

1. Samuel. The promised child is a miraculous gift to a virtuous woman. He serves as a prophet and a priest, but not a king—though he does anoint two of them.
2. The plea for a king. Israel cried out for a king just as people in a fallen condition cry out for a Savior. Jesus is seen in the desire and ultimately in the fulfillment.
3. David. The shepherd who killed a giant is something of a Messiah figure pointing to Jesus, his future descendant. Born in Bethlehem and given a promise of an eternal throne, David was Israel's prototypical king. One of Jesus' common titles is "son of David."
4. Solomon. His name is from the word shalom, or peace, wholeness, and fullness. The Messiah is called the Prince of Shalom in Isaiah 9:6.
5. Kingdom wisdom. Both Hebrew and Greek thought envision a personified logic or reason serving as an agent of creation. In Hebrew thought, it's wisdom (Proverbs 8-9, especially 8:22-31); and in Greek, it's logos (John 1:1-3, 14). This creative agent is specified as Jesus in Colossians 1:15-16.
6. The Temple. Just as the tabernacle was where God dwelled as His people journeyed to Canaan and lived initially in the land, so the temple in Jerusalem became His "home." Later, Jesus becomes the "place" where the holy presence resides. Now, since the time of Pentecost (Acts 2), the church (and individual believers in Jesus) are God's temple.

NOTES/JOURNAL

_____

_____

_____

_____

_____

_____

_____

_____

_____

_____

_____

_____

_____

_____

_____

_____

_____

_____

_____

_____

_____

LOOK AHEAD

It has been said that there are no second-generation believers. Everyone has to come to faith themselves for the first time. That's why much but not all of David's devotion is reflected in Solomon, and why little of Solomon's devotion is reflected in many future generations of kings. In fact, quite a few of the coming kings will turn almost completely to foreign gods. And not long after Solomon's death, the kingdom itself will split. And the battle for the hearts of the nation will continue.

OVERVIEW

God's people wanted a king, primarily because they wanted to be like the nations around them. This was the exact opposite of the calling God had given them to be distinct and set apart. And yet God agreed to grant their request (and let them experience the truth that every earthly monarchy comes with a cost).

The Israelites learned it isn't enough just to have a king; it's important to have the right kind of king. The first ruler of Israel, Saul, only looked the part; his heart wasn't right. When it was convenient and expedient, Saul obeyed God. But when he felt like compromising, he did that. As a result God tore the kingdom away from Saul and gave it to David, a young man with a passionate desire to honor God. For a while these two, the once and future kings of Israel, co-existed. In time, however, Saul grew envious, his desperate paranoia driving him to try repeatedly to kill David. Upon Saul's death, David ascended to the throne. His years of having to trust God while eluding Saul prepared him to rule. David followed God wholeheartedly but far from perfectly. In fact, a scandalous affair and deadly cover-up brought great grief to God, great shame to David, and much pain to his family and to the Israelite nation.

Young Solomon succeeded his father David. He honored God initially by praying for and governing with wisdom. He was given the great privilege of building Israel's glorious temple. He was blessed with peace. Over time, however, Solomon's heart for God cooled. He married foreign women who did not share his spiritual beliefs. Talk about a missed opportunity: the king with so much wisdom failed to consistently live by the things he knew to be true.

THE STORY: THE HEARTS OF THREE KINGS

When **1 Samuel** begins, the era of the judges and a corrupt priesthood are nearing their end. Through a desperate mother's prayers, God raises up a dedicated priest named Samuel who will preside over Israel's transition into monarchy. The first king, Saul, is physically imposing and seemingly courageous, but he forfeits his kingdom through casual disobedience and becomes unstable and manic. David survives a long exile from Saul, trusting God in caves and deserts and developing resourcefulness and character. A man after God's own heart, David writes many of the **Psalms** that display his love for God and his desire to build a temple and develop the nation's worship. But after David becomes king in **2 Samuel** (see also **1 Chronicles**), he commits a terrible series of sins that throw his kingdom into turmoil for years to come. Even so, God forgives David, blesses him, and promises to establish his throne forever. When his son Solomon ascends to the throne in **1 Kings** (see also **2 Chronicles**), the kingdom flourishes initially under his wisdom and wealth. Solomon writes numerous **Proverbs**, as well as an essay on disillusionment called **Ecclesiastes**. He is also either the author of or inspiration for a love poem, the **Song of Songs**, which has been a picture of marital and divine love for readers through the ages. But Solomon's compromises begin to erode the foundation of worship and obedience that David had laid. Multiple marriages to foreign wives serve to diminish his commitment to God. Solomon fails to finish well.

In short, Israel's king with no heart was replaced by a king with a whole heart who was followed by a king with a half-heart. Tragically, the king with the divided heart left behind a divided kingdom.

WATCH

In the world, success is often defined by wealth, power, status, influence, and accomplishments. In God's kingdom, success is a matter of the heart. As you watch, notice the effects of compromise. How does God respond to the hearts of His people? What consequences does He allow them to experience? What attitudes does He bless and support? What happens when we live passionately and purposefully toward Him?

VIDEO NOTES

_____

_____

_____

_____

_____

VIDEO REFLECTION/GROUP DISCUSSION

How did David handle his moral failure? How do we handle it today in our culture?

_____

_____

_____

_____

DIG DEEPER

The condition of our hearts doesn't show up in big, one-time decisions nearly as clearly as it does in the smaller, moment-by-moment choices we make. Who are we when no one is looking? How easily are we tempted to cut corners in our work, our relationships, our finances, our moral and ethical standards, and our worship and offerings to God? Are we going through the motions, putting on a show, practicing a religion, or living deeply and passionately toward Him? In the nuts and bolts of normal, daily life, how much of our hearts does He have? We may have to peel back some layers to see the true picture, and that's essentially what Scripture does for us in the stories of Saul, David, and Solomon, as well as the people before them like Hannah, Eli, and Samuel. In some cases, the picture is beautiful. In others, it isn't beautiful at all. But in every case, it will teach us something about ourselves.

SAMUEL

Hannah prayed for a significant blessing (a son) but offered an enormous sacrifice in return (giving the son back to God). God gave her Samuel. Hannah gave Samuel back to God. God used Samuel to transform a nation. What do you think was greater? God's gift or Hannah's sacrifice? Why? What's a sacrifice you've offered to God?

Read 1 Samuel 8:6-9. Why do you think God took Israel's desire for a king personally? What does this reveal to you about God's heart?

KING SAUL

Read 1 Samuel 15:20-26. Why didn't Saul's defense sway Samuel (or God)? Can you think of a time when you said the words of repentance even when your heart wasn't truly repentant?

"It is possible to obey God without loving Him, but it is not possible to love Him without obeying Him." Do you agree with this statement? Why or why not? Which is God more interested in: our love or obedience?

SAUL VS. DAVID

Read 1 Samuel 17:20-33. In what ways does this passage portray the differences between the hearts of David and Saul? What is the current state of your "heart for God"?

In 1 Samuel 24 and 26, David twice had opportunities to kill Saul, the man who had been zealously trying to kill him, yet David refused to touch "the Lord's anointed." What do these stories tell us about David's character? How might you have reacted in this same situation?

KING DAVID

Read 2 Samuel 6:12-23. In what ways is David's passion for God reflected in this story? What other concerns took a back seat to his worship? How is this a model for you?

David's famous sin with Bathsheba not only involved adultery but also a cover-up that included arranging for her husband's death. He later repented, but why did this sin not disqualify David from being king? from writing Scripture (several psalms after the event)? from being in the Messiah's lineage? How does this episode affect his reputation as "a man after God's own heart"?

KING SOLOMON

Because Solomon asked for wisdom instead of riches, a long life, and victories in battle, God gave him "all of the above." How does Solomon's request reflect God's heart? In what ways do your prayer requests reflect His heart?

Read 1 Kings 11:1-8. How does Solomon's behavior contradict God's heart? Which is a greater offense: that he violated God's law or that he violated the relationship? In what ways is our behavior a relational matter with God?

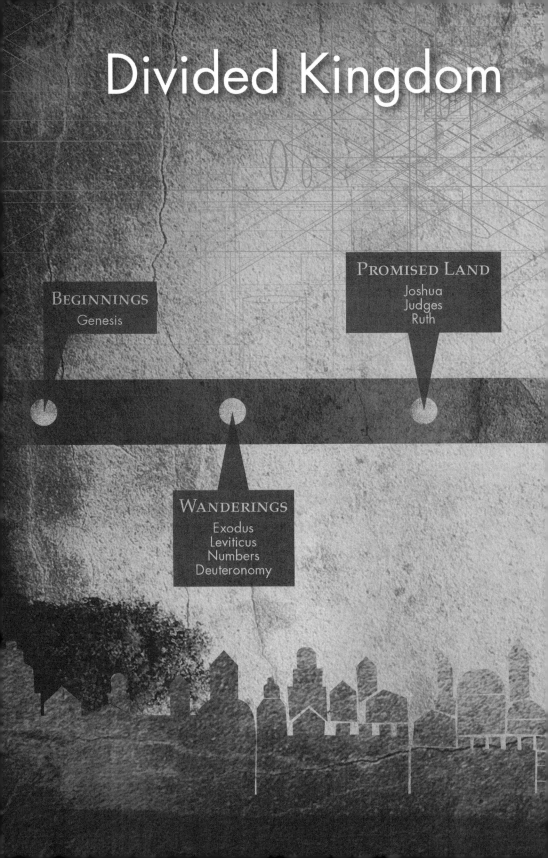

DIVIDED KINGDOM

2 Kings 12-25   Amos
2 Chronicles   Obadiah
10-36   Jonah
Isaiah   Micah
Jeremiah   Nahum
Lamentations   Habakkuk
Hosea   Zephaniah
Joel

UNITED KINGDOM

1 & 2 Samuel
1 Kings 1-11
1 Chronicles
2 Chronicles 1-9
Psalms
Proverbs
Ecclesiastes
Song of Songs

CAPTIVITY & THE COMING KINGDOM

Ezra
Nehemiah
Esther
Ezekiel
Daniel
Haggai
Zechariah
Malachi

Rift and Rebellion

1 Kings 12-14; 2 Chronicles 10-12

Read 1 Kings 12:16-33

*When all Israel realized that the king had refused to listen to them, they responded,
"Down with the dynasty of David! We have no interest in the son of Jesse."
(1 Kings 12:16 NLT)*

Solomon had worked the people hard and taxed them heavily in order to build and expand the kingdom of Israel. The result was glorious, but the cost had been painful. His son Rehoboam faced a choice: he could continue in his father's ways or ease the burden on the population. His older, wiser advisers from his father's generation urged him to ease off. His peers urged him to prove to the nation that he was just as authoritarian as his father. Rehoboam listened to his peers, and the result was a rebellion and secession by every tribe except Judah and Benjamin. Never again would all 12 tribes be united under one government. Solomon, the king of the divided heart, set the stage for a divided kingdom: nine tribes in the north referred to as Israel, and two in the south referred to as Judah (Benjamin joined with Judah soon after the split), and the Levites remained scattered throughout both territories. Just as God had said, most of the kingdom had been ripped from Solomon's son.

Worse than the political split was the spiritual rebellion that followed. Jeroboam, the king who led the north, didn't want the people of Israel to travel south to Jerusalem and its temple, since that was now considered foreign territory. So he set up an alternate worship system: different gods with their own altars, different feasts (but at the same time as Judah's so the people couldn't go to both), and different rituals. He established one shrine at the southern end of his territory and one at the far north. From now on, these kindred tribes would live separate lives. At times they would function as close allies, at times they would war against each other, but usually they would simply coexist.

So the nation called to be separate and distinct, holy to God and set apart to worship Him, was fractured and prone to give its worship indiscriminately to other gods in the region. And God would begin calling them persistently and passionately back to Himself.

REFLECTION

- At this point, God's plan seemed to be failing miserably. Why do you think He allowed the chosen nation to nearly forfeit its calling? Do you think it would have been different if He had chosen another nation instead? Why or why not?
- How is Jeroboam's "choose-your-own-religion" approach seen in our world?
- What attitudes tend to create division among people? What attitudes cultivate unity? Which do you tend to see most among Christians today? in your own life?

NOTES/JOURNAL

BOTTOM LINE
God allows us to experience the consequences of our own choices, even when those consequences are unpleasant and contrary to His will.

PRAY that God would show you any heart attitudes or actions that might be signs of drifting away from Him, or that might be disunifying to your family or church.

Good Kings, Bad Kings

1 Kings 15-22; 2 Kings 1-24; 2 Chronicles 13-35

Read 2 Kings 17:1-23; 2 Chronicles 34

"The eyes of Yahweh roam throughout the earth to show Himself strong for those whose hearts are completely His." (2 Chronicles 16:9 HCSB)

Over the next few centuries, there were 19 kings in the northern kingdom of Israel, and none of them were good. During the same time (plus an additional century after the Assyrians sacked Israel), there were 20 kings in the southern kingdom of Judah, and only eight of them were good (in varying degrees). Occasionally one of the southern kings would realize how far God's people had fallen and attempt reforms. Among the better kings were Asa, who banished shrine prostitutes from the land and even deposed his grandmother for being an idolater (and perhaps functioning as a pagan priestess); Jehoshaphat, the son of Asa who removed many but not all shrines, won a battle primarily through worship, and encouraged people to return to God; Hezekiah, who smashed sacred pillars, carefully obeyed the law of Moses, and desperately sought God's help in battle and in illness; and Josiah, who fought idolatry, repaired a long-neglected temple, and rediscovered the long-lost book of the law. God seemed to honor the good kings with longer reigns and broader support, and He allowed the reigns of evil kings to be filled with turmoil and strife. The covenant blessings and curses of Deuteronomy played out predictably in this era of the kingdom's history, yet not even those dire consequences produced any lasting heart change among the people of God. The fact is, when we humans are convinced our way is right, we tend to ignore or deny any evidence to the contrary. In the cases of Judah and Israel, sometimes they responded to divine judgment by trying even harder to appease their false gods. Stubborn hearts are hard to change.

Yet God kept looking for—and finding—faithful remnants. And He often spared them from the harshest consequences of the nation's sins. He kept His promise to support those whose hearts were completely His.

REFLECTION
- What does this era of Israel's history show us about the human heart? Why do you think we are so fickle with our loyalties, especially in our relationship with God?
- What challenges might the good kings have faced in trying to reverse the trends of their culture? In what ways is God prompting you to go against the grain of culture?
- Do you think God always protects faithful people from difficult circumstances? Why or why not? What does it mean for Him to show Himself strong on our behalf?

NOTES/JOURNAL

_____

_____

_____

_____

_____

_____

_____

_____

_____

_____

_____

_____

_____

_____

_____

_____

_____

_____

_____

BOTTOM LINE

Laws and programs cannot change hearts; only God can do that. But those who seek and ask will experience His support and find deep and lasting change.

PRAY for faithfulness to God, your church's impact on your community, and protection for Christians serving and living in hostile places in the world.

Elijah and Elisha

1 Kings 17-22; 2 Kings 1-13

Read 1 Kings 18:17-40; 2 Kings 2:1-14

Elijah went before the people and said, "How long will you waver between two opinions? If the LORD is God, follow him; but if Baal is God, follow him." But the people said nothing. (1 Kings 18:21 NIV)

Ahab and Jezebel stand out as perhaps the worst king and queen in the northern kingdom's history, primarily because of their open support for establishing Baal worship as the kingdom's official religion. Both could be manipulative, but Jezebel in particular, a priestess of Baal herself, attempted to eliminate all worshipers of Yahweh and recruit other priests and priestesses of Baal. So the prophet Elijah stepped on the scene and declared a drought, just as God's covenant stipulated for idolatry. And three years later, Elijah arranged a showdown on Mount Carmel between himself and the priests of Baal. Elijah built an altar for Yahweh. The priests of Baal built one for their god. The rules for this "battle of the gods" were simple. Each "side" would pray and whichever altar was struck by fire from heaven would prove the reality and superiority of its God/god. Elijah's altar burst into flames, of course, even though Elijah had first drenched it with water (for added effect). Baal was nowhere to be seen, and so while the priests of Baal were slaughtered, the people of Israel shouted their commitment to God.

Did this prompt Israel's leaders to turn the national religion back to the worship of the true God? Of course not. Stubborn hearts are hard to change. Jezebel was furious, and Elijah fled in fear, which then turned into depression. God led him back to Mount Sinai, back to the roots of the nation, to hear His voice once again. There were more faithful people in Israel than Elijah had thought, and one would succeed him as a gifted prophet.

That successor, Elisha, asked for a double portion of Elijah's spirit—a hard burden to bear, but a necessary one for the nation. Would he get it? After Elijah was taken up to heaven in a whirlwind accompanied by a chariot of fire, Elisha crossed back over the Jordan through parted waters and, over the course of his life, performed exactly twice as many recorded miracles as Elijah did. He reversed a curse on Jericho, raised a child from the dead, healed a Syrian general—a Gentile foreigner, of all people—and successfully asked God to strike an army with blindness, among other works and wonders. He and his mentor demonstrated that even in dry and dangerous times of rebellion and corruption, God's mercy is still given through those who are faithful to Him.

REFLECTION

- In what ways did Elijah put God's reputation, as well as his own, on the line? What was at stake if God had not struck his altar with fire? Do you think this kind of boldness is an exception or a model for us to follow? Why?
- What was God doing during this time to get His people's attention? What kinds of things has He done in your life to get your attention?

NOTES/JOURNAL

_____
_____
_____
_____
_____
_____
_____
_____
_____
_____
_____
_____
_____
_____
_____
_____
_____
_____
_____
_____

BOTTOM LINE

Even when His people seem spiritually deaf, God gets their attention and calls them back into fellowship with Him.

PRAY for a pure heart, for God to show you areas of compromise in your life, and for revival in our time.

Prophets Speak—and Write

Isaiah, Jeremiah, Hosea, Joel, Amos, Obadiah,
Jonah, Micah, Nahum, Habakkuk, Zephaniah

Read Isaiah 5:1-7; 11:1-10; Jeremiah 25:1-14; 29:10-14; Hosea 6

The LORD reached out his hand and touched my mouth and said to me, "I have put my words in your mouth. See, today I appoint you over nations and kingdoms to uproot and tear down, to destroy and overthrow, to build and to plant." (Jeremiah 1:9-10 NIV)

We don't know the author (or authors) of 1 and 2 Kings or 1 and 2 Chronicles. Thankfully, we have in those Old Testament books records of the powerful words and works of Elijah and Elisha. The two prophets themselves, however, didn't write down any of their prophetic messages, at least none that have survived. However, many later prophets did put their prophecies on parchment. Some of them prophesied to the northern kingdom of Israel to warn of the impending judgment (ultimately invasion and overthrow by Assyria), but many more prophesied to the southern kingdom of Judah to turn hearts back to God and to warn of judgment. More than a century after Israel was judged, Judah fell when the king of Babylon sacked Jerusalem and carried many of its people into exile. During the reigns of good kings and bad, God sent messengers to interpret events and declare His purposes. Beyond simply predicting the future, the prophets helped God's people see their circumstances through the lens of His perspective.

That wasn't always a clear picture. Mixed in among the true prophets were plenty of false ones who were quick to say words that evil kings and godless citizens wanted to hear. Not so with God's prophets. They made it clear that the nation's idolatry wasn't just disobedience, it was spiritual adultery. The leaders' corrupt and unjust practices weren't just a matter of bad judgment, they were affronts to God's character and His love for the oppressed. Merchants who cheated their customers, rulers who lied to their constituents, teachers who distorted God's truth, and, most of all, people who worshiped at pagan shrines and even sacrificed their children there—these were heinous offenders in the kingdom that was meant to reflect God's glory. According to the prophets, God's greatest desire was for people to turn back to Him and worship Him alone. If they wouldn't, He would be compelled to follow through with the consequences He had promised long ago. Even so, after their harsh and painful discipline, He would restore them. Beyond the suffering would be a future and a hope—and, one day, an unimaginably beautiful restoration of God's true kingdom forever.

REFLECTION

- If you had lived during the time of the divided kingdom, how would you have discerned between true and false prophets? What characteristics would you expect God's messages to have?
- Do you tend to think of God's challenge to either turn back to Him or experience judgment as words of love or words of anger? Why? In what ways has He spoken difficult but loving truths to you?

• In what ways is idolatry spiritual "adultery"? Why do you think God used such a graphic term?

NOTES/JOURNAL

_____

_____

_____

_____

_____

_____

_____

_____

_____

_____

_____

_____

_____

_____

_____

_____

_____

_____

BOTTOM LINE
God is vocal. He speaks to His people, and those who are listening can hear His voice.

PRAY for the ability to hear God's voice, and for the boldness to share His truth with a world that seems to prefer falsehood.

Judgment

2 Kings 25; 2 Chronicles 36; Lamentations

Read 2 Chronicles 36:11-21; Lamentations 1

Yahweh, the God of their ancestors sent word against them by the hand of His messengers, sending them time and time again, for He had compassion on His people and on His dwelling place. But they kept ridiculing God's messengers, despising His words, and scoffing at His prophets, until the Lord's wrath was so stirred up against His people that there was no remedy. (2 Chronicles 36:15-16 HCSB)

About 200 years and 19 kings after Solomon, the northern kingdom was invaded and overthrown by Assyria. In spite of the dramatic ministries of Elijah and Elisha and the words of later prophetic voices, none of the kings repented of their idolatry, and neither did the population as a whole except for brief moments. Just as God had said through Moses and Joshua centuries earlier, He would bring a distant nation against His people if they did not keep the covenant. He gave them plenty of time, but they did not turn back to Him. Assyria scattered them across their empire and resettled the land with their own people. Israelites who remained intermarried with these foreigners, creating a "mixed" breed called Samaritans who would be despised in later centuries by "pure" Jews.

Over a century later, Judah was also judged through a series of invasions by Babylon. Some Jewish leaders were taken to Babylon during this time; Ezekiel prophesied to the early exiles while Jeremiah prophesied in Jerusalem. In the third invasion, Jerusalem was destroyed and much of the population was killed or exiled. The siege lasted over two years, during which time people suffered from thirst and starvation. Despite unspeakably brutal conditions, the nation had not and would not turn back to God. He tried everything to get their attention—even national devastation and humiliation.

This was a major crisis in Israel's history. The covenant people would never be the same again. They would return to the land, trickling back for decades after they were allowed, but never again would they have the kind of kingdom they could have had if only they had remained faithful to the covenant. Their lack of love for God and the disobedience that resulted from it cost them more than they could have imagined.

REFLECTION

- Do you think the overthrow and captivity of God's people demonstrated God's rejection of them, His love for them, or His severe mercy to them? Why?
- Why do you think the people did not respond to God's messages to them through droughts, famines, defeats, and the prophets? Why were they so hard of hearing? What can we do to avoid the same problem?
- Why is it so important to God that His people know and love Him?

NOTES/JOURNAL

_____

_____

_____

_____

_____

_____

_____

_____

_____

_____

_____

_____

_____

_____

_____

_____

_____

_____

_____

BOTTOM LINE
God is serious about winning the love of His people, even if pain is part of the process.

PRAY for deeper love for God, for the kind of heart that responds in humility and quick obedience.

DAY 6-7 Jesus in the Divided Kingdom

The prophets are full of references to a coming King, some of them extremely well known. (Isaiah's prophecies of a child being born are notable examples.) Jesus is also behind the scenes in . . .

1. Elijah and Elisha. John the Baptist is described in the New Testament as an Elijah figure preceding Jesus. Elisha did many miracles foreshadowing the miracles of Jesus, and his name has the same meaning: "God is salvation."
2. Suffering Servant. Of the many pictures of the Messiah in the Old Testament, one of the most interesting is the Suffering Servant in several Isaiah passages. Isaiah 53, in particular, is a graphic portrayal of Jesus.
3. Victorious King. Messianic prophecies also depict a coming victorious king. Many Scripture commentators didn't know how to reconcile the victorious king and suffering servant passages, some suggesting perhaps two Messiahs would come. The New Testament presents one Messiah with two comings—once as a suffering servant, and finally as a victorious king.
4. Savior/Redeemer to come. Even the prophecies of harshest judgment against God's people are followed by passages of hope and promises of a future restoration. This restoration is often depicted in ultimate terms—a redemption that will undo all the brokenness of the fall.

NOTES/JOURNAL

_____
_____
_____
_____
_____
_____
_____
_____
_____
_____
_____
_____
_____
_____
_____
_____
_____
_____
_____
_____
_____

LOOK AHEAD

For God's people, no setback is final and no situation is hopeless. Even our worst circumstances are lined with opportunity and a promise of God's ability to heal, restore, and redeem. Or, as one of the prophets wrote, He can make up for all the years the locusts have eaten. Yes, He disciplines His children, and no discipline seems pleasant at the time. But it is never simply for the purposes of punishment or rejection. He is constantly calling us back into deeper knowledge of Him and into His purposes. Even in the hardest times, He has a greater plan.

OVERVIEW

When Solomon dies, he leaves the nation of Israel in the hands of his son Rehoboam. Yet the kingdom soon breaks apart—an event foretold by God due to Solomon's sins (and Rehoboam's political ineptitude). Rehoboam ends up ruling only two of the nation's 12 tribes; his kingdom comes to be known by the name of the larger tribe, Judah. The nine tribes to the north carry on under the name Israel (the tribe of Levi—the Levites—remained scattered all over). The northern kingdom was ruled for some two hundred years by a parade of bad kings, each one leading the people further from God. After many unheeded prophetic warnings, the northern kingdom succumbs to the invading Assyrian army. In the south, things are only a little better. Of the twenty different kings over a 350-year period, only eight of them are God-honoring leaders. In time, Judah also faces judgment—at the hands of the Babylonians. Just as God's covenant with Israel stipulated, allegiance to other gods brings devastating results.

THE STORY: GOD'S MESSENGERS

God sends numerous messengers (aka "prophets") to speak to His wayward people in both the northern and southern kingdoms. These bold spokesmen confront kings and religious leaders, delivering messages full of judgment, but also sprinkled with brief words of hope and subtle promises of a Redeemer to come. Behind all the doomy, gloomy language of the prophets, we see a God whose heart is broken over the unfaithfulness of people. Like a jilted lover, He is wounded and anguished over the fickle and faithless nature of His people. And yet He cannot and will not let them go. He keeps calling and wooing and urging them to come home.

Two well-known prophets from **1** and **2 Kings**, Elijah and Elisha—as well as many lesser known prophets—didn't provide any written contributions to Scripture, but many after them did. Though it's difficult to determine the dates of some, the prophets in the divided kingdom era (also covered by **2 Chronicles**) seem to break down as follows:

- Prophets to the northern kingdom before the Assyrian invasion: **Hosea** and **Amos**
- Prophets to the southern kingdom before (and up to) the Babylonian captivity: **Isaiah, Jeremiah, Lamentations (written by Jeremiah), Joel**, **Micah, Habakkuk, Zephaniah**
- Prophets to other nations: **Jonah** and **Nahum** (Nineveh of Assyria); **Obadiah** (Edom), who likely prophesied after the fall of Jerusalem

There are other scriptural prophets, of course, but some of them minister mainly during the captivity or afterward. Most of these listed above are specifically called to warn their listeners of impending judgment, even though God knows the messages will often go unheeded. Their messages nearly always have immediate implications, but many look beyond the scope of the moment and into God's lasting and eternal purposes. And they nearly always offer reason for hope amidst the devastation.

WATCH

Scripture speaks often of having "ears to hear." This concept comes up in Isaiah and is echoed often in the ministry of Jesus. Few people had ears to hear during the era of the divided kingdom, and their inattentiveness to God proved to be a dangerous condition. As you watch the video, think about the various ways people respond or refuse to respond to God. What does it take for Him to get our attention? How can we know when He wants to correct us? What can we do to avoid the need for His correction in the first place? And, applying these questions to you personally, how can you know if you have ears to hear?

VIDEO NOTES

_____

_____

_____

_____

VIDEO REFLECTION/GROUP DISCUSSION

What circumstances or situation are you facing in your life where you're beginning to doubt or not fully understand the timing of God?

_____

_____

_____

_____

DIG DEEPER

Many people see in the Old Testament an angry God, not a God of love. But anger has been called "a secondary emotion" that is usually rooted in some deeper hurt. Is it possible for human beings to hurt God? According to the prophets, He has at times felt betrayed, wounded, and rejected by His people. Israel's and Judah's worship of other gods was often portrayed in terms of adultery—a treacherous violation of intimacy. And according to the long-ago words of Deuteronomy 6:5, His primary purpose for His people is that they love Him. Our disobedience is not a matter of failing His behavioral standards; it's a matter of our weak and flawed love for Him. As you read about and discuss the history of Israel and Judah during the centuries of the divided kingdom, consider it not only from the perspective of the kings, prophets, and citizens of the land, but also from the perspective of a God who loves His people with a passionate and jealous love.

RIFT AND REBELLION

Read 1 Kings 12:26-30. In what ways did Jeroboam's misplaced priorities, short-term thinking, and impulsive decision-making shape Israel's future? What big decisions are you facing that could affect others deeply and what can you learn from Jeroboam?

Have you ever been part of a church split or some other big public conflict that separated close Christian friends?

GOOD KINGS, BAD KINGS

At times during the era of the divided kingdom, the book of the law—the history and instructions revealed by God through Moses—was lost and forgotten, a relic of ancient history. Why do you think no one kept the faith going during these times? In what similar ways do you wrestle with forgetting or neglecting God's Word?

Why do you think there were some good kings in the south but none in the north? Why do you think you have some "good spiritual days" and some "bad spiritual days"?

Why do you think this part of the Bible—the history of kings and the prophets—is one of the least-read portions of Scripture today?

ELIJAH AND ELISHA

Read 1 Kings 17:1. How is Elijah's statement consistent with God's previous revelation? If someone today said these words, how do you think we would respond to him? Why?

In 2 Kings 2:9, Elisha asked for a double portion of Elijah's spirit. Why did Elijah call this "a difficult thing" (2:10)? What are the costs of having a significant calling in God's kingdom? What are the benefits? Would you ask for a double (or even a single) portion of Elijah's spirit? Why or why not? What are the costs—and benefits—of having a significant calling in God's kingdom? Whose spirit would you like to have a double portion of and why?

PROPHETS SPEAK—AND WRITE

Scripture refers to many people as prophets, from Abraham to members of the New Testament church. Why do you think God sent so many prophets to His people during this period of history? What was so urgent about His message? Do you believe God is sending prophets today?

Read Isaiah 6:9-13. How did God expect His people to respond to His messages? Are you moved by and do you respond more readily to thunderous messages of rebuke or thoughtful messages of encouragement? Why?

JUDGMENT

Why do you think God judged His own chosen people? What could they have done to avoid His judgment? How does God want *us* to respond to Him?

Captivity & the Coming Kingdom

BEGINNINGS
Genesis

PROMISED LAND
Joshua
Judges
Ruth

WANDERINGS
Exodus
Leviticus
Numbers
Deuteronomy

DIVIDED KINGDOM

2 Kings 12-25
2 Chronicles 10-36
Isaiah
Jeremiah
Lamentations
Hosea
Joel
Amos
Obadiah
Jonah
Micah
Nahum
Habakkuk
Zephaniah

UNITED KINGDOM

1 & 2 Samuel
1 Kings 1-11
1 Chronicles
2 Chronicles 1-9
Psalms
Proverbs
Ecclesiastes
Song of Songs

CAPTIVITY & THE COMING KINGDOM

Ezra
Nehemiah
Esther
Ezekiel
Daniel
Haggai
Zechariah
Malachi

Captivity

Ezekiel, Daniel

Read Ezekiel 6:1-10; 37:1-14; Daniel 1, 9

"This is what the Sovereign LORD says: I will end the captivity of my people; I will have mercy on all Israel, for I jealously guard my holy reputation!" (Ezekiel 39:25 NLT)

Most of the northern kingdom had been taken into exile by the Assyrians, but Assyrian practice was to weaken conquered peoples by assimilating them. The result was that even the people who remained in the land did not remain distinct, mixing with Assyrians who settled there. The tribes of the north were never discernible again and are often referred to today as the lost tribes of Israel.

Babylonian practice was to take conquered peoples into captivity, so Judah remained distinct even in a foreign land. According to 2 Chronicles 36:21, this captivity was prophesied to last 70 years—long enough to make up for all the Sabbath rests the people had neglected. But an official decree about 50 years later gave permission for the Jews to begin to return and rebuild. In the early years of this exile, Ezekiel and Daniel prophesied to the captives in Babylon. Ezekiel did so even before Jerusalem had fallen, and Daniel began his forced service in Babylonian courts as a young boy and continued at least until the time of the return. During that period, the Babylonian Empire was overthrown by the Persians, whose policies toward exiles eventually allowed the captives to return. A decree by Cyrus made that possible five decades after the destruction of Jerusalem.

Though the captivity may seem to have been nothing more than divine punishment of the Jewish people, God had a larger agenda. He was preparing them to represent Him not only in the ancient land of promise but also in the far reaches of civilization. He who does all things well was accomplishing more than one purpose, working all things—even His people's rebellion—toward a good end. This wasn't a unique event; it's His pattern. Even in our worst predicaments, He sees the end of the story and promises that it can be good. The process may be painful, but the result is better than we hoped. Our trials are more than just trials; they are the means to a satisfying end.

REFLECTION

- In what ways is the situation of Daniel and many other exiles—trying to remain faithful to God in a foreign land—a picture of our lives today? What challenges does our culture present to those who want to have godly attitudes and behavior? How can we remain faithful in a hostile environment?
- How is our perspective of God affected when we experience hardship or His discipline? What can we do to keep a right perspective of Him and our situation in those times?
- Are any situations, patterns, habits, relational issues, or sins making you feel captive? If so, what steps can you take toward freedom? How does God promise to help you?

NOTES/JOURNAL

_____

_____

_____

_____

_____

_____

_____

_____

_____

_____

_____

_____

_____

_____

_____

_____

_____

_____

_____

BOTTOM LINE

God's will for His people is freedom, not captivity. He gives us grace to endure and faith to trust Him for deliverance.

PRAY for people you know who are making crucial life decisions.

Return

Ezra 1-2, Daniel 9; Zechariah 1-2

Read Ezra 1; Daniel 9:1-19

"O my God, lean down and listen to me. Open your eyes and see our despair. See how your city—the city that bears your name—lies in ruins. We make this plea, not because we deserve help, but because of your mercy." (Daniel 9:18 NLT)

When Cyrus issues his decree allowing the Jewish exiles to return to their homeland, a group of settlers prepared to journey back to Jerusalem. Priests, Levites, and former tribal leaders gathered necessary supplies. Articles of gold and silver, many of which had been taken from the temple by Nebuchadnezzar years before, were given to them to return to the land. In all, the first wave included several thousand returnees, and subsequent waves brought many more. Many stayed where they were—they had learned the language, built homes, and, to some degree, adapted to their new culture. Still, a substantial remnant made the journey to begin again. And this time they were determined to be faithful to God.

When they arrived back home, some settled in villages around Jerusalem while others returned to their towns. They seemed to know they had deserved the harsh discipline they had received, but they were also filled with hopes of future prosperity and a kingdom that reflected the glory of God. Would things be different this time? They had a lot to learn. Younger generations were unfamiliar with the language, and few remembered the meaning of true worship and the details of God's law—after all, idolatry and neglect of the law were the reasons behind their exile in the first place. Temple practices were a faint and distant memory. Not only that, the temple was still in ruins. Rebuilding and re-establishing a God-honoring nation would be a long process.

Nevertheless, the people returned home, committed to worship God in truth; to rededicate themselves to learning His Word; to cling together as a community of faith; and, whether in Jerusalem or in the far reaches of the empire, to influence the world for the glory of the one true God. They would spend the next few centuries learning how to do that, and they wouldn't always get it right. But at least their hearts were back in the right place.

REFLECTION

- How would you have felt if you had been one of the Jews who returned to the land you had left as a child? How would you have felt if you were one of the younger ones who had never seen the homeland?
- What expectations would you have for life in a once-devastated city? What hopes would you have for God's restoration of your people?
- Though we can never return to the past, we can return to commitments from the past. Are there commitments, relationships, or perspectives from the past that you might need to restore? If so, what steps can you take to do so?

NOTES/JOURNAL

BOTTOM LINE

God always looks forward. Even when we feel stuck in the past, He offers a fresh start.

PRAY for a fresh start with God, and for a wholesale turning to God in your city, state, and country.

Restoration

Ezra, Nehemiah, Haggai, Zechariah, Malachi

Read Ezra 3:8-13; Nehemiah 1:1–2:8; 8:1-3, 9-12; Zechariah 8

"The glory of this present house will be greater than the glory of the former house," says the LORD Almighty. "And in this place I will grant peace." (Haggai 2:9 NIV)

God's mission is not simply to get us back to where we were. He is a restorer and a renewer. His goal is to take everything in the past and craft it into something better, stronger, and deeper than before. So when the first wave of exiles unpacked their bags in Jerusalem, it was only the beginning. The returnees would construct a new temple, better than before. They would pursue a new understanding of God and His ways, deeper than before. They would build a new community, stronger than before.

Zerubbabel, the governor, and Joshua, the high priest, set about the task of leading the returnees in rebuilding the foundation of the temple. Those who remembered Solomon's temple wept, perhaps because the former glory seemed lost. Haggai, however, prophesied a greater glory, a temple filled with God's presence that would surpass even Solomon's experience. Ezra and Nehemiah were among later waves of exiles (the whole process of "returning" took some 100 years). Ezra was a scribe and a priest, an expert in God's law. His goal was to rebuild the people by teaching them God's truths. Nehemiah had been the cupbearer to the king of Persia when he heard of the rundown condition of Jerusalem. He had appealed for royal assistance to rebuild the city's walls. That was his agenda. Together these two leaders accomplished much! They oversaw the rebuilding of the walls of Jerusalem—in only 52 days! They had the law of Moses (i.e., the Torah) read aloud to the people. (They even had it translated for those Jews who had been born and reared in Babylonian captivity and thus had never learned Hebrew!) They reinstituted the Jewish feasts. Their efforts brought great joy to the people.

But their efforts and accomplishments were not unopposed. Local adversaries, who did not want the Jews back in the land, attempted to harass, discourage, deceive, and slander the leaders and the people. Zerubbabel and Joshua had resisted and overcome opposition years before, and Ezra and Nehemiah would do the same by remaining focused on the task, shutting out the voices of the enemies, guarding against attack and deception, and remembering their calling and God's promises. They persevered; God overcame. He was making all things new.

REFLECTION
- Nehemiah encouraged those who wept by telling them that the joy of the Lord was their strength (8:10). What do you think he meant by this? How can we have God's joy in difficult or painful situations?
- Each of us is in a restoration process from our fallen nature (see Philippians 1:6). In what ways is God transforming us? What is His ultimate purpose for us? (Hint: See Galatians 4:19.)

- How are we opposed in our God-given calling? What can we do to overcome the opposition? What lessons can we learn from Nehemiah's response to his adversaries?

NOTES/JOURNAL

_____

_____

_____

_____

_____

_____

_____

_____

_____

_____

_____

_____

_____

_____

_____

_____

_____

_____

BOTTOM LINE

God doesn't only redeem; He restores. And even when we face fierce opposition, He will complete the process if we remain focused on Him.

PRAY for God's restoration process in your life, and for the faith to trust that He is at work even when all seems lost. Ask Him to quiet all the opposing voices and for the grace to hear His voice above the rest.

The Scattered

Esther

Read Esther 3:8-11; 4:13-17; 7-8

"If you keep quiet at a time like this, deliverance and relief for the Jews will arise from some other place, but you and your relatives will die. Who knows if perhaps you were made queen for just such a time as this?" (Esther 4:14 NLT)

Far away from Jerusalem in the Persian city of Susa, King Xerxes impulsively deposed his queen. After some time, he held a beauty contest to find a new queen, and a young Jewish woman named Hadassah was chosen and given the Persian name Esther. When ethnic rivalry flared between her cousin Mordecai and the king's right-hand man, Haman—a descendant of the Amalekites, whom Saul had been told to destroy centuries earlier—a sinister plot to wipe out the Jews began to take shape. Haman crafted an edict for genocide, got the king to agree to it, and set a date for the destruction of the Jews. But Esther, whose ethnic background was still secret, was in a perfect, yet dangerous position to influence the king. If he listened to her, her people could be saved. If he didn't, she and her people would die.

In a plot filled with comic twists and ironic turns, Esther revealed her ethnic identity and convinced the king to spare her people; Haman's plot against Mordecai and the Jews was turned back against him; and Jews across the empire were actually strengthened rather than destroyed. Mordecai became the king's new right-hand man, and God's deliverance—even though God is never mentioned—was celebrated throughout Persian lands. This celebration became the festival of Purim, which is still observed today as the happiest of all Jewish holidays. And in later dispersions and persecutions—the Roman destruction of Jerusalem that sent Jews scattering away from their homeland, as well as the Holocaust of the 20th century—the story of Esther has served as profound encouragement that God is always watching out for His people wherever they are.

That was a needed message in Esther's time, as it is in ours. No matter where we are, even if we are far from home and out of our comfort zone, God orchestrates situations and circumstances for our good. He is sovereign, and His eye is on His people.

REFLECTION

- If you had been in Esther's situation, would you have interpreted the events as a crisis or an opportunity? as God's displeasure or an occasion to strengthen you? Why?
- Why do you think the writer of Esther left it for the reader to decide whether God was in the story or not? How is this like the story of our own lives?
- In what situation(s) do you need God to turn the tables on adversity? What role might you, like Esther, need to take in that process?

NOTES/JOURNAL

_____
_____
_____
_____
_____
_____
_____
_____
_____
_____
_____
_____
_____
_____
_____
_____
_____
_____
_____
_____

BOTTOM LINE

God defends His people, turning extreme adversity into greater strength.

PRAY for boldness for believers worldwide who have been sovereignly placed in strategic positions of influence. Pray that they will both show and share the love of Christ with those in power.

The Coming Kingdom

Daniel 7-13; Zechariah 9-13

Read Malachi 2:17–3:4; Zechariah 3:3-5

"For My name will be great among the nations, from the rising of the sun to its setting. Incense and pure offerings will be presented in My name in every place because My name will be great among the nations," says Yahweh of Hosts.
(Malachi 1:11 HCSB)

God is vocal. He has always spoken to His people to give them direction, encouragement, and correction. But He seems to speak more often during times of transition, when next steps are critical and His people need energy and insights to fulfill His purposes. So when the temple project was sluggish, when the people were disheartened, and when corruption was creeping back into the worship life of the newly restored community, God spoke through His prophets again.

But He didn't just speak about the current situation. He gave them glimpses of the geopolitical future and the greater kingdom to come. Daniel not only saw angelic warriors doing battle on behalf of God's people, but he also saw successive empires eventually giving way to an everlasting kingdom. Zechariah saw visions of God's current work among the returnees rebuilding the temple, but he also saw a hostile world one day surrounding Jerusalem, with God defending His land and establishing everlasting peace and prosperity among His people. Malachi saw a need for correction for current attitudes and actions of the Jewish people, but he also saw God suddenly coming to His temple one day and sending a messenger to prepare the way. The prophets—and the Jewish people through them—got glimpses of traumatic judgments followed by a glorious future.

Among all these visions stands a divine figure. Ezekiel and Daniel saw Him as a glorious Son of Man. Zechariah saw Him as a Shepherd and a King riding on a donkey. Malachi saw Him as a Sun of Righteousness with healing in His wings. These would be encouraging and necessary images; the next four centuries would be seen as an era of divine silence. God is always active, of course, and likely always speaking. But Scripture would include no written prophecies until the time of this divine figure's advent—when an even greater restoration of God's creation would be revealed.

REFLECTION

- God revealed to Daniel the progression of empires over the next few centuries. What does this tell us about His sovereignty? On what basis can we trust Him even in the midst of international chaos and global conflict?
- Why is it important to know that God speaks to us during times of transition? How can we position ourselves to hear His voice?
- What is God's ultimate purpose for this world? How do you see your own life fitting inside this larger plan?

NOTES/JOURNAL

BOTTOM LINE

God's plan is bigger than we can imagine at any given moment. A true perspective is always more comprehensive than our own.

PRAY for a greater awareness of and a deeper involvement in God's global, eternal plan. Ask Him to show you how you can use your God-given abilities and passions to make an eternal difference in this world.

Jesus in the Captivity and the Coming Kingdom

There is perhaps no better picture of a person in need of rescuing than a captive in exile. Not surprisingly, God gave the captives, as well as those returning to the land, plenty of pictures of a Rescuer. We can see Jesus behind the scenes in . . .

1. Daniel. When Daniel's three friends were thrown into a blazing furnace for refusing to worship at the king's statue, a fourth man was seen among the flames with them—one who had the appearance of a god (Daniel 3). And the Son of Man in Daniel's vision of the Ancient of Days (Daniel 7) was a title Jesus used for Himself.
2. Ezekiel 36:26-27. In both Ezekiel and Jeremiah, God promises to replace hearts of stone with a new heart and a new spirit—a promise hinted at by Jesus and reiterated in New Testament writings.
3. Joshua and Zerubbabel. In various places, Joshua the high priest (same name as Jesus) and Zerubbabel are described in messianic terms, pictures of a greater one to come.
4. Zechariah. In 9:9, Zechariah prophesies a King riding on a donkey; in 12:10, Jerusalem grieving for one whom they have pierced; and in 13:7, sheep scattering when the Shepherd is struck. All of these (among other references) point to the New Testament portrait of the Messiah.
5. Malachi. A messenger prepares the way, and the Lord—the messenger of the covenant—suddenly comes to His temple (3:1). In chapter 4, the prophet Elijah is sent before judgment, and the Sun of Righteousness rises with healing in His wings.

NOTES/JOURNAL

_____
_____
_____
_____
_____
_____
_____
_____
_____
_____
_____
_____
_____
_____
_____
_____
_____
_____
_____
_____
_____

LOOK AHEAD

The Old Testament is the story of God's work. It begins with creation and takes us through the history of the people He has called to love Him. But it isn't only a history; the entire collection of books points us forward. It prompts us to look ahead to what He is doing, not only in this world but ultimately in His eternal plan. It answers many questions about where we came from and why we were created, but it prompts many other questions that will not be answered until the true King returns to His kingdom. In the meantime, we can be fulfilling our kingdom purposes now as those who are redeemed, restored, renewed, and always looking ahead to a greater glory.

OVERVIEW

The Babylonian Empire is overtaken by the Persian Empire during Judah's captivity, and when Cyrus becomes king, he issues an edict allowing the Jewish exiles to return to their homeland and rebuild. They will still be governed by the empire, of course; they are not allowed to establish their own independent country. But at least they can begin to recreate the society and culture distinctive to their people. The younger ones will need to relearn the language, and the worship and sacrificial systems, having been based in the Jerusalem temple, will have to restart from scratch. Slowly, they can try to recapture the glory of their former kingdom and align themselves with the heart of the God they betrayed.

So how does one return to God? Spiritually, it isn't difficult; He welcomes His people back with open arms. But to reestablish Jerusalem as a worship center based on the law of Moses requires leadership and a priesthood, a functioning temple, a secure city, and an invested community. There are parallels in our worship lives today; we need many of the same attributes the returnees exhibited. But God is zealous about the hearts of His people and enables them to draw close to Him.

THE STORY: COMING HOME

During the captivity, **Ezekiel** prophesies to the early exiles, and **Daniel** has a long ministry in the courts of Babylon and Persia. Both see dramatic visions that reveal what God is doing during this tumultuous time and what He plans to do in the near and distant future. They are voices of hope in an almost-hopeless era.

At the prophesied time, an edict permits the exiles to return home. Many remain where they are, but Zerubbabel, a descendant of a former king of Judah, and Joshua the high priest lead the first wave of returnees. **Ezra**, a scribe and expert in the law, comes in a later wave and leads the return to God's Word. **Nehemiah**, a contemporary of Ezra, weeps over the deterioration of Jerusalem and returns to both oversee the rebuilding of its walls and to develop the unity of the people. **Haggai, Zechariah,** and **Malachi** prophesy in very distinct ways during the time of restoration following the exile. At times they encourage diligence in rebuilding efforts and in keeping the law. At other times, they both hear and speak words from God about His ultimate purpose for His people in centuries to come. Meanwhile, among those still scattered throughout the far reaches of the empire, a Jewish girl named **Esther** becomes Persia's queen and is able to use her influence to thwart a genocide planned against her people. No matter how distant geographically, culturally, or spiritually God's people are, Scripture portrays Him as carefully watching over them to strengthen their hearts and to preserve a lasting remnant.

WATCH

Almost everyone has regrets, but not many people know what to do about them. Scripture gives us powerful examples of God's people coming back from the brink of destruction, even when their desperate circumstances were the result of their own mistakes. As you watch the video, try to draw parallels between the national history of Judah and your own personal history. In what areas of your life do you need God's restoration? What challenges and obstacles do you face in rebuilding your life? What help does He provide? Most of all, notice His support of those who return to Him and accept His warm welcome back into His arms.

VIDEO NOTES

_____

_____

_____

_____

_____

_____

VIDEO REFLECTION/GROUP DISCUSSION

When you find yourself far away from God, what specific steps can you take to return to Him?

_____

_____

_____

_____

_____

_____

DIG DEEPER

Coming face to face with our sins is never easy, but it's necessary if we want healing and restoration. God forgives us, but we can't move forward without honesty about where we've been. Not only is this true for God's chosen people in the Old Testament, it's true for each of His people today. But just as He does with us today, God not only restores His people after the exile; He is actually putting them in a better position to accomplish His purposes. In the days of the united kingdom, He drew people from around the world to see His glory. But with His people scattered around the world, the stage is set for a much broader display of His glory one day. As you discuss God's ways with His people, notice that His redemption is always more than a consolation prize. It's a setup for an even greater opportunity.

CAPTIVITY

Read Psalm 137, an honest reflection of Jewish sentiments in captivity. What feelings does it describe? Can you relate? Why or why not? What aspects of God's perspective seem to be missing in this psalm?

Both Ezekiel and Daniel saw overwhelming, hard-to-decipher visions of God during the captivity. Why do you think God revealed Himself so openly during this time? If you were suffering in exile in a distant land because of your own sins, what attributes of God would you need to see most clearly?

RETURN

Daniel realized from reading Jeremiah's prophecies that the time for Judah's return was near. Why do you think he prayed so desperately for the release of the captives if God had already foretold it? What does this tell us about the need for and effectiveness of our prayers?

Read Psalm 126, which depicts Judah's return from captivity. In what ways is this psalm a reflection of God's purposes for all of us? In what ways have you experienced the truths of this psalm? What feelings or longings does it stir in you?

RESTORATION

Read Ezra 3:10-13. Why were some of the people weeping while others were joyful? Are you more likely to focus on your past or to focus on your future? Why?

Read Zechariah 8:2-3. In what ways is this passage surprising? How does God feel about His people? What does He intend to do for them? Do you think this is an accurate reflection of His heart toward us today? Why or why not?

THE SCATTERED

The book of Esther is a story of how the Jews were delivered from extinction, written about those who were scattered across the empire and for their benefit. It does not mention God, nor does it stress His instructions for His people (dietary laws or feasts and Sabbaths, for example) like other writings of this era do. Why do you think it's so different from the words written to the returnees to Jerusalem? What can its story tell us about God without mentioning Him?

What does Mordecai's statement in Esther 4:14 tell us about God's sovereignty? about human free will? about how His sovereignty and our free will interact? Do you have any examples of how God worked in and through your actions to accomplish something you never could have foreseen?

THE COMING KINGDOM

Read Haggai 2:7 and Malachi 3:1. What concept do these verses have in common? According to these verses, what do human beings desire? How does God fulfill that desire in you?

Why do you think there were 400 years without written, scriptural prophecy after the Old Testament writings?

BOOKS OF THE OLD TESTAMENT

- **GENESIS:** The story of beginnings—of creation, of the human story, of God's chosen people (through Abraham, Isaac, Jacob, and Joseph), and of His redemption plan.

- **EXODUS:** The deliverance of God's people from captivity in Egypt through the Passover and Red Sea, the covenant agreement at Mount Sinai, and instructions in the wilderness, including the Ten Commandments.

- **LEVITICUS:** Laws for Levites and priests, and the nation's offerings and feasts.

- **NUMBERS:** Life in the wilderness, with all its temptations, doubts, challenges, and need for dependence, provision, and guidance.

- **DEUTERONOMY:** A second expression of the law for a new generation—and a call to love God completely.

- **JOSHUA:** The entrance into the Promised Land and taking the territory He has given.

- **JUDGES:** A cycle of falling away, suffering the consequences, crying out to God, and being delivered—again and again for four centuries—while everyone does what is right in his own eyes.

- **RUTH:** Even in a rebellious time, God can write a love story that pictures His compassion and redemption.

- **1 SAMUEL:** Out of a lawless era, God raises up Samuel to replace a corrupt priesthood and David to replace an unfaithful king. But as long as Saul is king, he pursues David to kill him.

- **2 SAMUEL:** The story of David's kingship, including his successes and a major moral failure that results in turmoil.

- **1 KINGS:** Solomon becomes king and builds the temple his father longed to see. After his death, the kingdom splits into north and south.

- **2 KINGS:** After years of evil kings and national idolatry, God judges Israel through an Assyrian invasion. Over a century later, He judges Judah through the Babylonians.

- **1 CHRONICLES:** The history of Judah, with a focus on David's reign, is retold after the Babylonian captivity.

- **2 CHRONICLES:** Solomon builds the temple and the palace, and his successors attempt to reform Judah until the time of the captivity.

- **EZRA:** The exiles begin to return to Jerusalem to rebuild the temple and the city and to rededicate themselves to God and His Word.

- **NEHEMIAH:** Years after the temple has been rebuilt, the walls of Jerusalem are still in disrepair. Against much opposition from local antagonists, Nehemiah leads a focused effort to restore the city.

- **ESTHER:** In the Jewish dispersion, a sinister plot arises that would massacre all Jews. But the Persian queen reveals her Jewish background and thwarts the genocide.

- **JOB:** No one knows when it was written or by whom, but this timeless story of a man's suffering raises life's biggest questions and lets the answers rest in the hands of God.

- PSALMS: Israel's worship book, full of praises, songs, laments, prophetic words, prayers, blessings, and odes.
- PROVERBS: A collection of wisdom and sayings written largely by Solomon.
- ECCLESIASTES: Toward the end of his life, Solomon realizes his vast wealth, successes, and pleasures were ultimately unsatisfying—and life under the sun appears futile.
- SONG OF SONGS: A love poem written either by, about, or for Solomon gives us rich pictures of marriage and, metaphorically, of God's love for His people.
- ISAIAH: Long prophecies in Judah interpreting the times, warning of future judgment, and picturing God's eternal plan and the Messiah at the center of it.
- JEREMIAH: The weeping prophet foretold Jerusalem's destruction and had to live through it, all while being persecuted simply for telling the truth.
- LAMENTATIONS: The saddest book in the Bible laments the fall of Jerusalem from among the rubble.
- EZEKIEL: Among the early exiles in Babylon, Ezekiel sees God, warns of Jerusalem's devastation, and foretells the future restoration and ultimate kingdom.
- DANIEL: Daniel serves in foreign courts during the Babylonian-then-Persian exile, seeing sweeping visions of God, His defense of His people, and His global plan.
- HOSEA: Like an unfaithful, adulterous wife, God's people had betrayed Him. And Hosea had to act out the prophetic picture by marrying a prostitute.
- JOEL: Though a plague of locusts—or an invasion by a locust-like, swarming army—has devastated the land, God will restore lives and even pour out His own Spirit on His people.
- AMOS: A prophet from the south confronts the north about the purity of its worship, its ethical and moral behavior, and its treatment of the oppressed.
- OBADIAH: A judgment against Edom for rejoicing over the destruction of Jerusalem.
- JONAH: The reluctant prophet is sent to Nineveh, a hostile Assyrian city, to preach repentance because, unlike the prophet himself, God has compassion on it.
- MICAH: The southern kingdom is not living up to its potential in representing God's character. Micah rebukes injustices, warns of judgment, urges repentance, and offers hope.
- NAHUM: Judgment is coming to Nineveh, the enemy of Israel, and it will fall.
- HABAKKUK: In words directed toward God, the prophet asks why God allows evil—and uses an evil nation to chastise His own people. Even so, he chooses to rejoice in God.
- ZEPHANIAH: Judgment is coming to the whole earth, and only those who trust in God will remain.
- HAGGAI: The returning exiles must prioritize the rebuilding of the temple. God will keep His promises, but His people must restore their worship.
- ZECHARIAH: God is jealous for the love of His people, and Zechariah's visions urged them to give it passionately. They also foretold peace to Israel and all nations.
- MALACHI: Integrity, right relationships, and heartfelt devotion are important to God. He purifies His people and will one day come to them in His temple.

CONTINUE YOUR

JOURNEY

You've completed *God's Grand Story* and you know God and His story so much better now. But where do you go from here? Whether you want to continue your journey individually or with your family, Sunday school class, or small group, we've got the next steps ready for you.

BIBLICAL RESOURCES

For more resources visit **walkthru.org**

Churchwide Campaign
God's Grand Story

Bibles & Books
Daily Walk Bible
Great Rescue Bible
One Year Devotionals

Devotional Magazines
Daily Walk, Closer Walk,
Tapestry, indeed, YW (Students)

Small Group Resources
World Religions
90 Days Thru the Bible
Story Thru the Bible

Small Group DVD Series
Crucible (Life of David)
Detour (Life of Joseph)

Bible Teaching Tools
Bible Flashcards, Coloring
Books, & Apps

Pastor & Teacher Resources
The Daily Walk Sermon Series
The 7 Laws of the Learner/
The 7 Laws of the Teacher

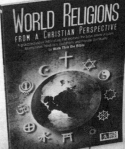

GLOBAL IMPACT
Learn more at **walkthru.org**

Get involved in a global ministry that impacts lives and communities around the world.

The vision of Walk Thru the Bible is to develop a global network of pastors and Christian leaders who make life-changing biblical resources available worldwide.

Our global network has helped change lives, preserve families, address social needs, and inspire churches in more than 100 countries. Reaching their communities in dramatic ways, our global partners are helping to change the world, one person at a time, through the power of God's Word.

LIVE EVENTS
Experience the Bible like never before!

Walk Thru the Bible Premier Live Events:

- Walk Thru the Old Testament
- Walk Thru the New Testament

Max Lucado:
"Your team hit a home run with our Walk Thru the Bible Live Event..."

Why Host a Walk Thru the Bible Live Event?

- Removes the intimidation of the Bible
- Provides the big picture of the Bible through a fun, exciting experience
- Presented in person by a dynamic Walk Thru the Bible instructor
- 75% of participants commit to daily Bible reading

View the Live Event promo at walkthru.org/live-events

Learn more about all of our live events at www.walkthru.org/live-events

- **Thru the Bible (4 events)**
- **Marriage and Family (4 events)**
- **Leadership and Teaching (3 events)**
- **God's Grand Story (churchwide campaign)**

About **Walk Thru the Bible**

Walk Thru the Bible ignites passion for God's Word through innovative live events, inspiring biblical resources, and a global impact that changes lives world-wide . . . including yours.

Known for innovative methods and high-quality resources, we serve the whole body of Christ across denominational, cultural, and national lines. We partner with the local church worldwide to fulfill its mission, communicating the truths of God's Word in a way that makes the Bible readily accessible to anyone. Through our strong global network, we are strategically positioned to address the church's greatest need: developing mature, committed, and spiritually reproducing believers.

Our live events and small group curricula are taught in more than 45 languages by more than 80,000 people in more than 100 countries. More than 100 million devotionals have been packaged into daily magazines, books, and other publications that reach over five million people each year.

Wherever you are on your journey, we can help.

Walk Thru the Bible
www.walkthru.org
1.800.361.6131

What is the **God's Grand Story** series?

Walk Thru the Bible has developed a family of resources designed to creatively communicate God's Grand Story. By better understanding the big picture, our passion for God's Word is often sparked. Our goal with this series is simple: develop dynamic resources that can be used by individuals, small groups, and entire congregations to better understand the big picture of the Old and New Testaments.

The God's Grand Story series is available as:
- A six-week Church-wide Campaign—for all ages
  Includes a live event kick-off, daily readings, Bible studies, sermons
- A Family Devotional Guide:
  The Best Story...Ever!
- Group/individual Bible Studies for Adults and Students
  Including Jesus in the Old Testament and several more

More resources are being developed! Learn more: **www.thegrandstory.org**

Leader's Notes are located at **www.walkthru.org/ggsot**

You've Stepped into **God's Grand Story** . . .

SHARE WHAT YOU'VE LEARNED AND HELP CHANGE THE WORLD.

Helping people everywhere live God's Word isn't just a mission statement to us—it's our passion. We know the key to life change is a passion for God and His Word, and we work in over 100 countries to bring His truth to the world.

When you see what your partnership with us can accomplish, it will reignite that passion in you too. When you see His truth prompting ministries to AIDS victims and orphans, influencing leaders in government and education, or reaching millions in "closed" countries, it's easy to start seeing doors of opportunity everywhere and to dream big. Taking a walk can change the world.

FIND OUT HOW AT
WWW.WALKTHRU.ORG

WALK THRU THE **BIBLE**®

TAKE A WALK. CHANGE THE WORLD.

Prayer Requests

Prayer Requests

Prayer Requests

Prayer Requests

Prayer Requests

Prayer Requests